HANDBOOK OF
PARANORMAL POWERS

HANDBOOK OF
PARANORMAL POWERS

DISCOVER THE SECRETS OF
MIND READERS, MEDIUMS, AND MORE!

BRIAN HAUGHTON

RUNNING PRESS
PHILADELPHIA • LONDON

ISBN 978-0-7624-4089-4
Library of Congress Control Number: 2010928918

This book was designed and produced by
Quintet Publishing Limited
6 Blundell Street, London N7 9BH

Project Editor: Asha Savjani
Editorial Assistant: Holly Willsher
Additional Text: Carly Beckerman
Designer: Ian Ascott
Illustrator: Bernard Chau
Art Editor: Zoë White
Art Director: Michael Charles
Managing Editor: Donna Gregory
Publisher: James Tavendale

Running Press Book Publishers
2300 Chestnut Street
Philadelphia, Pennsylvania 19103-4371
Visit us on the web!
www.runningpress.com

Printed in China by 1010 Printing Ltd.

CONTENTS

INTRODUCTION

uring November of 2009, newspapers and Internet news sites in the UK were full of the story of 62-year-old Alan Power, formerly of the Greater Manchester Police. In October 2008, Power was fired from his job as a specialist police trainer and co-ordinator after just three weeks, apparently for claiming that psychics should be used to help solve crimes. Power stated he had experienced ghostly visions from childhood and believed that psychics could contact people after their death, and so assist the police in the investigation of crimes.

Power initially presented a successful case in defending his right to protection from religious discrimination in the Employment Appeal Tribunal. However, the Greater Manchester Police were adamant that Power, who was at the time studying for a PhD in parapsychology, was fired for something entirely different. The police insisted that it was Power's improper conduct during training sessions, and a series of complaints about his behavior at other police colleges, that prompted the dismissal. At the final hearing, the employment appeal tribunal decided to listen to the Greater Manchester Police and accepted that Power had been dismissed for reasons other than his spiritualist beliefs.

Photograph by Professor Barrett and Gordon Salt showing a ghostly vision.

BELIEF IN THE SUPERNATURAL

	2001 GALLUP POLL	FARHA-STEWARD STUDY
Psychic/spiritual healing	54%	56%
ESP	50%	28%
Haunted houses	42%	40%
Satanic possession	41%	40%
Telepathy	36%	24%
Communication with the dead	28%	16%
Reincarnation	25%	14%
Clairvoyance/prophecy	24%	32%
Channeling	15%	10%

At the time of his firing, Power had been a member of a spiritualist church for almost 30 years. Spiritualism is a faith group, which according to the 2001 Census, is the eighth largest in Britain, with 32,000 or so people claiming membership. This is a surprisingly high figure for a group supporting what is essentially a belief in the reality of paranormal phenomena. In the US, a 1989 national survey found that 67 percent of the adult population believed they had experienced extrasensory perception (ESP), and a staggering 20 million Americans had undergone some kind of psychic experience. Census results from the US between 1990 and 2005 show that belief in the paranormal is widespread and consistent. In 1990, 26 percent of the population believed in the reality of

Opponents argue that there are natural and scientific explanations for what are often perceived as supernatural phenomena.

How do we explain such beliefs and where do they originate? Skeptics insist that most of them can be put down to the influence of the media.

Currently, interest in supernatural powers is at an all-time high, partly because of the profusion of television, professional magicians, movies, and shows with paranormal themes, and the Internet, with its online psychics, healers, and tarot readers. Movies such as *The Sixth Sense* (1999) and *The Others* (2001), television series such as *Medium*, *Heroes*, and *Ghost Whisperer*, as well as "reality" television shows such as *Ghost Hunters* and the UK's *Most Haunted* series, are hugely popular all over the world.

But this interest in what lies outside of the reality we interpret via our five senses goes much deeper. Supernatural phenomena capture our imagination mainly because they appear just beyond the limits of

Above: The Sixth Sense, a film written by M. Night Shyamalan is about a boy who communicates with spirits that don't know they're dead.

clairvoyance (the power to perceive objects, physical events, persons, or images without using the ordinary five senses). In 2000 this had risen to 30. In the UK, a 2006 survey undertaken by *Reader's Digest Magazine* revealed that more than half of Britons believed in psychic powers such as mind reading and premonitions (visions of the future).

A 2006 poll of over four hundred college students by researchers Bryan Farha of Oklahoma City University and Gary Steward of University of Central Oklahoma found that seniors and graduate students were more likely to believe in supernatural phenomena than college freshmen. When the two researchers compared their results with a 2001 US Gallup poll, they found a fairly consistent pattern (see table opposite).

Above: Circe from Homer's *Odyssey* was a goddess of magic whose music could turn men into beasts.

Imitation model of an alien from Roswell, New Mexico, in 1947.

our present knowledge and understanding. The human belief that certain individuals possess psychic powers is extremely ancient. Homer's *Odyssey* (written around the eighth century BCE), for example, is full of incidents illustrating these supernatural abilities, as is the Bible.

Throughout history, seers, prophets, magicians, holy men, mystics, shamans, and occultists have been credited with a vast range of supernatural powers. All of these abilities can generally be placed under the heading of either extrasensory perception (ESP): the ability to acquire information by apparently paranormal means; or psychokinesis (PK): the movement of physical objects by the mind without use of physical effort.

This book takes an in depth and thought-provoking look at these inexplicable abilities, and includes case studies of the enigmatic characters who have displayed them as well as scientists who have investigated them.

Science and the paranormal have always enjoyed an awkward relationship. This is due to the fact that there is so little physical evidence for unexplained human powers, and also because of the number of charlatans and hoaxers in the field. Parapsychology's connections with fringe subjects such as UFOs, astrology, the Yeti/Sasquatch, ritual magic, witchcraft, and the occult also does not mix well with serious scientific research. This is why the majority of scientists have shown at most a mild curiosity, and often some annoyance, at those professing psychic, healing, or other strange powers. Furthermore, any researcher delving into strange powers is faced with the problem that by definition, paranormal abilities are not accepted as real by science. If they were accepted, they would be referred to as "natural," rather than "supernatural."

Despite these problems, scientific studies of the supernatural have taken place, many taking the form of studies of paranormal beliefs, rather than actual physical research and experiments (see opposite). As in

PRIZES FOR EVIDENCE OF PSYCHIC POWERS

ORGANIZATION	PRIZE MONEY	DETAILS
Abraham Kovoor's challenge	Rs.100, 000 (Sri Lankan Rupees) (approx. $890 in 1963)	For anyone able to demonstrate supernatural powers under controlled conditions.
Association for Skeptical Enquiry (ASKE) (UK)	£13,000 (approx. $20,000)	For proof of psychic powers.
Australian Skeptics	AU$100,000 (approx. $91,000)	For proof of psychic or paranormal powers.
Center for Inquiry West (CFI)	$50,000	For a demonstration of paranormal ability, scientifically tested on stage.
Finnish Association of Skeptics	€10,000 (approx. $13,500)	For anybody in Finland able to produce paranormal phenomena under satisfactory conditions.
Indian Skeptic 100,000 Paranormal Challenge	100,000 rupees (approx $2,000)	For anyone demonstrating any psychic, supernatural, or paranormal ability under satisfactory observing conditions.
North Texas Skeptics	$12,000	For anyone able to demonstrate any psychic or paranormal power under scientifically valid observing conditions.
Québec Skeptics	$10,000	For any astrologer able to demonstrate their craft according to formal scientific experiment.
Scientific American	Two $2,500 awards (in 1922)	(1) For the first person able to produce an authentic spirit photograph. (2) For the first medium to produce a "visible psychic manifestation."

Based on information at http://www.skepdic.com/randi.html. Dollars are US unless otherwise stated.

LO!
by CHARLES FORT
AUTHOR OF "THE BOOK OF THE DAMNED"
Illustrated by ALEXANDER KING

Introduction by
TIFFANY THAYER

Acclaimed by

THEODORE DREISER
"Charles Fort is the most fascinating literary figure since Poe. His books thrill and astound me."

BOOTH TARKINGTON
"Anyone interested in unorthodoxies, who enjoys having his imagination staggered and mind dazzled, should read this vigorous and astonishing book."

HARRY ELMER BARNES
"A most amazing production."

BENJAMIN DECASSERES
"Charles Fort has the mystical, psychic penetration of a Blake and a Leonardo."

JOHN COWPER POWYS
"I am struck sharply and starkly by the curious genius of Charles Fort."

BEN HECHT
"He has delighted me beyond all men who have written books in this world."

(see table on previous page). The best known and most controversial of these "challenges" was that offered by the James Randi Educational Foundation (JREF). The prize offered by the JREF was US$1,000,000 to be paid out to anyone who could demonstrate a supernatural ability under agreed scientific testing criteria. In March 2010, after offering the money for 12 years with no successful challengers, the JREF prize was discontinued. Indeed none of the prizes listed in the table on page 11 have so far been claimed. Of course this does not mean that no one will ever claim one of these prizes. All it would take is for one person to demonstrate a single, reproducible example of ESP or PK, to turn science on its head and prove that there really are supernatural powers beyond those shown in comics, novels, television shows, and movies.

folklore studies, it is the collection of anecdotes by paranormal researchers like Charles Fort (1874–1932), that has provided the largest proportion of the evidence for people claiming abnormal abilities. Scientific testing of individual "powers" is discussed in the relevant chapters of this book, but although such experiments have been taking place for at least a century, not one person has been found who is able to consistently demonstrate any psychic power under scientifically valid observing conditions. Believers may object to this assertion and claim that, for example, Israeli psychic superstar Uri Geller has proven his abilities time and time again. However, Geller remains a controversial subject, whose powers are still believed by some (arch skeptic, James Randi, for example) to be nothing more than the result of sophisticated sleight of hand.

In 1922, the journal *Scientific American,* offered one of the first prizes to anyone who could prove supernatural powers under controlled conditions. Since this time many organizations have offered what are often substantial prizes for proof of psychic phenomena

Above: James Randi, investigator and demystifier of paranormal and pseudoscientific claims.

DEFINITIONS

⚙ASTRAL BODY

The ethereal counterpart or double which exists alongside the physical body as a vehicle of the soul or consciousness.

⚙ASTRAL PROJECTION

The act of separating the astral body from the physical body.

⚙AURA

A luminous emanation said to surround human beings and objects which certain people are able to see using psychic powers.

⚙BILOCATION

The ability to exist simultaneously in two locations.

⚙CHANNELING

The process whereby a person (the "channeler") serves as a medium through which a spirit entity or guide purportedly communicates with the living.

⚙CLAIRVOYANCE

The ability to see objects, people, or events that cannot be perceived by the five senses.

⚙DIVINATION

The attempt to foretell the future or discover hidden knowledge about an object, event, place, or person by supernatural means.

⚙DOWSING

Searching for underground water, minerals, or other buried or hidden objects by using a dowsing rod or pendulum.

⚙EXTRASENSORY PERCEPTION (ESP)

The reception of information independently of sight, hearing, feeling, touch, or taste.

⚙MEDIUMSHIP

A form of communication with spirits of the dead or entities from other realms. A person thought to have the power to communicate with these spirits or entities is known as a medium.

⚙PARAPSYCHOLOGY

The scientific study of the evidence for paranormal phenomena such as telepathy, clairvoyance, and psychokinesis.

⚙PRECOGNITION

Knowledge of something in advance of its occurrence.

⚙PSI

A collective name for all paranormal or psychic phenomena.

⚙PSYCHIC HEALING

The alleged ability to bring physical healing to a person using only supernatural powers.

⚙PSYCHIC SURGERY

The alleged means of healing or removing diseased tissue using bare hands or simple instruments, painlessly and without injury to the patient.

⚙PSYCHOKINESIS

The process of moving or affecting material objects using the mind only, without any physical contact with the object.

⚙PSYCHOMETRY

The ability to obtain knowledge about an object or person connected with it, using touch.

⚙REMOTE VIEWING

The ability to gather information about a distant or unseen target using ESP.

⚙RETROCOGNITION

ESP of past events.

⚙SCRYING

Also called crystal gazing. A type of divination whereby a person gazes at an object with a reflective surface (usually a crystal ball, bowl of water, mirror, or candle) until prophetic visions appear or hidden knowledge is revealed.

⚙TELEPATHY

Communication between two or more minds by means other than the known senses.

THE SIXTH SENSE

The sixth sense is the ability to acquire or transmit information through means other than the five known senses. It involves an as yet unexplained interaction between the mind of one person with that of another or with the material world. During the process, physical barriers such as locked doors and brick walls, as well as time and distance, are apparently disregarded by the mind as if they did not exist.

EXTRASENSORY PERCEPTION

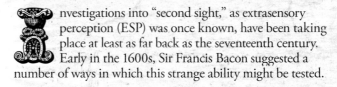

nvestigations into "second sight," as extrasensory perception (ESP) was once known, have been taking place at least as far back as the seventeenth century. Early in the 1600s, Sir Francis Bacon suggested a number of ways in which this strange ability might be tested.

One of the methods Bacon put forward was to test the claimants using a deck of cards. He recommended that investigators should note the proportionate amount of accurate guesses, or "hits," as to the correct suit or number of the next card made by those claiming second sight. Similar tests using a pack of cards were carried out in the 1880s by French psychologist and psychical researcher Charles Richet.

The term "extrasensory perception" was coined by parapsychologist Joseph Banks Rhine (1895–1980). Rhine carried out pioneering investigations into inexplicable human abilities at Duke University, North Carolina, beginning in the late 1920s. Along with his wife Louisa, Rhine pursued extensive statistical research into ESP at Duke until his death in 1980. Throughout his long career, Rhine devised experiments for his subjects to undergo in his search to demonstrate ESP under controlled laboratory conditions.

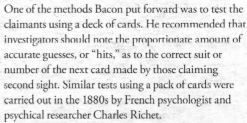

Sir Francis Bacon was one of the earliest people to suggest testing claims of ESP.

The best known of Rhine's experiments was a test using a set of 25 "Zener" cards. These cards, designed by Rhine's Duke University colleague, Dr. Karl Zener, were akin to an ordinary set of playing cards but each was numbered (1–25) and carried one of five easily visualized symbols—star, cross, square, circle, and wavy lines. Rhine would test students to find out whether any of them could guess the symbol on the cards correctly at a rate significantly higher than chance expectation. If the participant consistently

American parapsychologists Louisa and Joseph Rhine.

TYPES OF SECOND SIGHT

scored higher than five correct guesses in each run of 25 cards, it would suggest that there was some kind of hidden power involved—possibly ESP.

Nowadays, the term ESP, sometimes known as the "sixth sense," has come to embrace many of the best known so-called paranormal abilities which have been attributed to psychics, prophets, and mediums over the centuries. The most commonly studied of these types of ESP are telepathy, clairvoyance, and precognition, but retrocognition, certain aspects of psychic mediumship, channeling, auric sight, automatic writing, psychometry, medical intuition, dowsing, scrying, astral projection, remote viewing, and animal communication are all forms of ESP.

Right: A girl, using a planchette, receives a message by automatic writing.

HOW TO

TEST FOR ESP

ESP is the reception of information independently of sight, hearing, touch, smell, or taste. The best way to test for it, therefore, is to see whether the subject is able to provide information about a scene, sound, object, or person, with no prior knowledge or contact. Because of the possibility that subjects may guess accurately by pure coincidence, it is a difficult one to prove either way. Statistically, however, it has been shown that some people have a much higher accuracy rate than others, leading us to the conclusion that they might possess ESP.

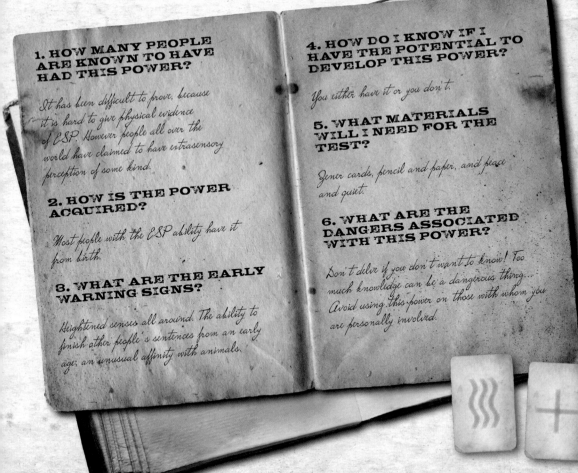

1. HOW MANY PEOPLE ARE KNOWN TO HAVE HAD THIS POWER?

It has been difficult to prove, because it is hard to give physical evidence of ESP. However people all over the world have claimed to have extrasensory perception of some kind.

2. HOW IS THE POWER ACQUIRED?

Most people with the ESP ability have it from birth.

3. WHAT ARE THE EARLY WARNING SIGNS?

Heightened senses all around. The ability to finish other people's sentences from an early age; an unusual affinity with animals.

4. HOW DO I KNOW IF I HAVE THE POTENTIAL TO DEVELOP THIS POWER?

You either have it or you don't.

5. WHAT MATERIALS WILL I NEED FOR THE TEST?

Zener cards, pencil and paper, and peace and quiet.

6. WHAT ARE THE DANGERS ASSOCIATED WITH THIS POWER?

Don't delve if you don't want to know! Too much knowledge can be a dangerous thing... Avoid using this power on those with whom you are personally involved.

TEST

GUESSING CARDS

The easiest way to identify whether you have any latent ESP abilities is to use a set of numbered Zener cards. These can be purchased from New Age stores. Statistically, random guessing in this test will produce on average 5 correct answers from every 25 cards. If you consistently to score higher than five correct answers after many trials, there may well be ESP at work!

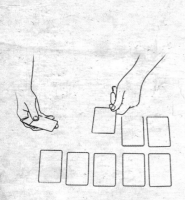

[1] Lay out the 25 Zener cards face down on a table in five rows with five cards in each row.

[2] Concentrate on each card, working from cards 1 to 25, for a few moments until the symbol you think it bears (star, cross, square, circle, or wavy line) appears in your mind.

[3] Write down the symbol you see and the card's number on a piece of paper.

[4] Turn the cards over and check your answers.

[5] Shuffle the cards thoroughly and start over again.

MATTHEW MANNING

English psychic and healer Matthew Manning was born in 1955, and according to accounts in his numerous books, he has demonstrated an astonishing range of paranormal abilities, including psychokinesis, retrocognition, auric sight, astral travel, automatic writing and drawing, and in more recent times, healing.

While still a child away at boarding school, Manning had an out-of-body experience where he apparently managed to astrally project himself back into his Cambridgeshire home; his mother felt his presence and he saw the inside of his house, though physically he was lying on his bunk bed in his school.

If he could do this, Manning reasoned, why not try to astrally project himself into the past?

While walking in a trance-like state, Manning saw an unknown boy approaching him. The boy was surrounded by a pear-shaped aura of colors that vanished as he walked past.

Back at home one weekend he lapsed into a trance-like state. After half an hour he could hear a woman's soft voice—she identified herself as Henrietta Webbe, who had died in 1673 and had lived in the house. Other "spirits" that had lived in the house came through and eventually Manning found himself witnessing a scene from 1731 when the house had just been rebuilt.

Shortly after this, while Manning was writing an essay for school, he became stuck for something to write. Suddenly his pen hand went down onto the paper and began to write incomprehensible sentences in a strange, scrawled handwriting, definitely not his own. He later tried this again in the company of six school friends and was soon receiving messages from someone, albeit very confused and unintelligible ones. Manning continued to write these messages, the communications becoming more coherent as time went on. Most of them seemed to be from "spirits" who had either died unpleasantly or who did not know they were dead. Manning also

began producing automatic writing in languages and scripts completely unknown to him, such as Greek and Arabic. But there was more to come.

One evening as Manning was walking on the school campus he saw a boy approaching him whom he didn't know. Manning had drifted off into an almost dream-like state while walking and

Manning demonstrates his healing technique.

noticed to his astonishment that the boy was surrounded by a pear-shaped "aura" of colors that resembled heat waves. These colors then vanished and the boy walked past. Manning soon discovered that he could switch his powers "on" and "off" like an electric light.

MATTHEW MANNING

Matthew Manning, faith healer, tries to heal a patient.

If he "switched on," as if he was about to start automatic writing but didn't actually do so, he could see auras surrounding people. He found that certain colors seemed to denote a personal trait in the individual—for example a fiery, temperamental character showed red as the main color, but if the person was also kind and generous then this red might be bordered by blue or purple. It seemed that the aura was particularly clear when it surrounded a person with psychic abilities, and weak around those who were ill; he also noticed that a darker shadow surrounded diseased parts of the person's body.

During the summer of 1971, Manning spent a lot of time carrying out automatic writing, mainly communicating with the "spirit" of a man named Robert Webbe, who in 1731, had built the front of the house where the Mannings lived, and had died shortly afterward in 1733. In the written communication Robert seemed not to realize he was dead and saw himself as owner of the house despite the presence of the Manning family. He was also bewildered at modern day (1970s) prices and the presence of "horseless carriages" (cars), and thought Manning was taking him for a fool. But there were some discrepancies in dates and personality in Robert Webbe's communication, and after a time it became clear to Manning that he was in fact communicating with two people—Robert Webbe senior, who had died in 1713, and Robert Webbe junior, who had built the house.

Another development was the appearance of signatures on the walls in various types of handwriting, again apparently from departed spirits. When pencils were left in a locked room, scratching noises were heard suggesting the action of writing, though this would not happen when anyone was in the room watching. In one particular week in 1971 more than five hundred signatures—some dated—appeared on the walls of Matthew's bedroom. The room had been locked and some of the signatures were written in inaccessible places such as on the ceiling and even on the lampshade.

Automatic writing received by Matthew Manning in 1972.

You should not really indulge in this unless you know what you are doing. I did a lot of work on automatic writing when I was alive and I could never work it out. No one alive will ever work out the whole secret of life after death. It pivots on so many things: personality, condition of the physical and mental bodies. Carry on trying though because you could soon be close to the secret. If you find it no one will believe you anyway.

The signatures were believed to represent people from Matthew's village who had lived from the fourteenth to the nineteenth centuries, some of whom were subsequently traced through parish registers.

Some of the inspiration for the signatures on the walls of Manning's room and the writings of Webbe must have come from Manning's research into his village history for a school history project in 1970, and also from finding the name "John Webbe 1731" scratched into a brick on the outside wall of the house. Manning amassed a lot of information on the Webbes and attempted to create a family tree for them—but there was a still a lot missing. As soon as he began to write out the notes on the Webbe family, Webbe began his communication, suggesting that he could fill in the gaps.

In April 1972 Manning received another automatic writing message, this time purportedly from Frederick William Henry Myers (1843–1901), pioneer psychical researcher and one of the founders of the Society for Psychical Research.

Those skeptical of Manning's claimed abilities are justifiably suspicious of the lack of reliable sources for his paranormal abilities beyond his own accounts. It is true that Manning has been tested and examined by reputable scientists, but the results of these tests are not presently available. Nowadays Manning claims he has learned to channel his "psychic energy" solely into healing.

SEE ALSO

ESP **Pages 16–21**
Automatic writing
Pages 96–102

TELEPATHY

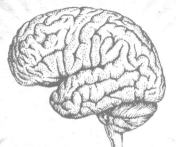

The word "telepathy" comes from the Greek *tele*, "distant," and *patheia*, "feeling," so it means literally, "distance feeling." Considered a form of ESP, telepathy is the direct transference of thought from one person (the sender) to another person (the receiver) without using normal sensory channels of communication, or instruments of any kind. Modern mystics, New Agers, and psychics all claim that telepathy is a latent power within all humans that only needs to be developed to show extraordinary results.

There are various types of telepathy, including the communication of feelings, the communication of emotions or images, and the communication of words. More commonly known as mind reading, telepathy is said to be most frequent among those with strong emotional bonds, such as identical twins. There is a large amount of anecdotal evidence for twin ESP, where one twin experiences a physical sensation of something involving extreme emotion or trauma that their twin is undergoing, such as a serious accident, heart attack, or labor pains.

Although scientific experiments into telepathy have been conducted for more than a century, the results remain controversial, and thus the existence of telepathy is scientifically unproven. The term "telepathy" was introduced in 1882 to replace the earlier expression "thought-transference," by the English classical

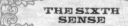

scholar Fredric William Henry Myers, a founder of the Society for Psychical Research (SPR). The vast majority of work by the SPR regarding telepathy, however, consisted of gathering a vast number of anecdotes, some of which were published in 1886 as the two-volume work *Phantasms of the Living*. In 1917, psychologist John Edgar Coover of Stanford University conducted a series of tests using playing cards on subjects claiming telepathic powers. However, Coover did not consider the results of the experiments significant enough to prove the existence of telepathy.

Rhine's experiments into ESP at Duke University, beginning in 1927, are discussed on page 17. In his first book, *Extra-Sensory Perception* (1934), Rhine controversially stated that he had carried out over 90,000 trials, and so believed that he was justified in concluding that ESP was "an actual and demonstrable occurrence."

Above: Carl Sargent conducts a test with a subject in a ganzfeld experiment.

Left: Daryl Bem, US parapsychologist and author of a report on the ganzfeld experiments.

There has been much criticism that Rhine was far from systematic in all of his experiments, and attempts to duplicate his results from these "ESP trials" at Princeton (New Jersey), Johns Hopkins University (Maryland), Colgate University (New York), Southern Methodist University (Texas), and Brown University (Rhode Island), all met with failure.

Between 1974 and 1981, 42 "ganzfeld experiments" ("ganzfeld" is German for "entire field") were carried out, the results of which, when published, were hailed as proving the existence of ESP. The tests were carried out by Daryl Bem, a Cornell University psychologist, and Charles Honorton, a parapsychologist from the University of Edinburgh. The technique involved in ganzfeld experiments was devised by Wolfgang Metzger (1899–1979) in the 1920s and 1930s, and requires a "sender" and a "receiver."

The experiments involved placing the subject (the "receiver") in a padded, darkened, and soundproof cubicle. The subject's eyes were then covered with halves of ping-pong balls, large headphones were placed over their ears, and the room was bathed in a red floodlight. White noise was then fed through the headphones into their ears. The receiver was thus deprived of most sensations. In another cubicle, the "sender" was shown randomly selected still photos and/or videotaped film sequences and asked to mentally send one (the "target") to the receiver. The receiver then reported whatever images came into their mind and attempted to identify, from a group of (usually four) pictures, the one closest to what the sender was trying to transmit to them via telepathy. If the receiver chose the correct image it was scored as a "hit."

Apparently the ganzfeld experiments produced extremely positive results, with subjects scoring a hit rate of about 35 percent, well above the expected chance rate of 25 percent. According to Charles Honorton, these results represent some of the strongest

Blackmore also objects to the fundamental premise of not only the ganzfeld experiments, but of much parapsychological research: that certain mental states, such as the dream state, the hypnotic state, a sensory deprivation state, the meditative state, and some drug-induced states are more conducive to PSI. Blackmore believes there is no evidence to back up this assumption.

Furthermore, Hyman discovered statistical anomalies in the original ganzfeld experiments, and posited that the results of the experiments could be put down to methodological errors. Nevertheless, many parapsychologists stand by the results of the ganzfeld experiments as providing the most convincing proof yet for the existence of telepathy and ESP.

Above: Susan Blackmore, English psychologist and psychical researcher.

scientific evidence for telepathy ever obtained. Indeed the results of Honorton's experiments were published in 1994 in a major psychology journal, co-authored by Cornell University psychology professor Daryl Bem, (*Psychological Bulletin*).

But not all researchers are so enthusiastic about Honorton's results. English writer and psychologist Dr. Susan Blackmore, and Ray Hyman, Professor Emeritus of Psychology at the University of Oregon, have objected to the fact that in some of the studies soundproof rooms were not used; so that when a video was playing the receiver could have heard it.

HOW TO

TEST FOR TELEPATHY

1. HOW MANY PEOPLE ARE KNOWN TO HAVE HAD THIS POWER?

It's difficult to say, but it is one of the most commonly reported supernatural powers, especially among twins.

2. HOW IS THE POWER ACQUIRED?

Telepathy is a latent power within all humans and is waiting to be developed, rather than acquired.

3. WHAT ARE THE EARLY WARNING SIGNS?

Repeatedly having "gut feelings" about people and events which turn out to be correct.

4. HOW DO I KNOW IF I HAVE THE POTENTIAL TO DEVELOP THIS POWER?

If you are particularly sensitive to the thoughts and feelings of others and have strong willpower you may have the potential to develop it.

5. WHAT MATERIALS WILL I NEED FOR THE TESTS?

Five objects of the same type but different colors (such as pens, rubber bands, sheets of paper, paper clips) for the "send and receive" test.

6. WHAT ARE THE DANGERS ASSOCIATED WITH THIS POWER?

Exhaustion from too much mental effort. Make sure you take breaks between experiments.

TEST 1

OBJECT TELEPATHY

[1] Prepare five objects of the same type but different colors—pens, rubber bands, sheets of paper, or paper clips, will do.

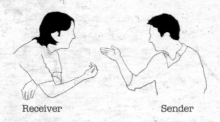

Receiver   Sender

[2] Sit down with another person and decide who will be the person who sends (the "sender") and who will receive (the "receiver").

[3] Relax, and center yourself with breathing exercises and/or meditation. Try to concentrate on the exercise, blocking out all other thoughts from your mind.

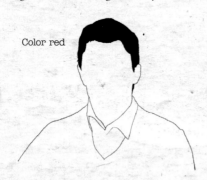

Color red

[4] The sender chooses a color in their mind and starts the telepathic transfer by saying the word "begin."

[5] Meanwhile, the receiver concentrates hard and attempts to connect with the mind of the sender to see if they can pick up on what is being sent.

Color yellow?

[6] The receiver then says out loud what he/she believes the color to be.

[7] The sender says whether or not the color was correct (a simple "yes" or "no" will suffice).

[8] If the response is "no," the sender keeps transmitting thoughts of the same color for up to another five minutes.

[9] The sender then chooses another color (or the same one again) says "begin," and sends the color.

[10] Take a break, and when you start again reverse the roles of sender and receiver to see if the success rate is higher/lower.

TEST 2

TELEPHONE TELEPATHY

Telephone telepathy occurs when, for no apparent reason, you are thinking of a friend or relative who then happens to phone at that moment; or you hear the phone ring and somehow "know" who it is, even though you were not expecting them to call. Unorthodox biologist, Rupert Sheldrake, carried out a series of experiments at Goldsmith's College, London, to investigate this phenomenon, where he obtained statistically significant results persuading him that something more than chance was at work. In Sheldrake's experiments at Goldsmiths, the subjects were correct over 40 percent of the time in 571 trials, a result which he believes completely rules out the possibility of coincidence.

Although most scientists believe telephone telepathy to be complete "pseudoscience," there is a simple experiment you can perform to put it to the test.

[1] First you will need to select one person to receive and four people to be send. These people should either be members of your family or people you know well.

[2] Ensure that the receiver is in a different location to the senders.

[3] Randomly select one of the senders to make a call to the receiver at a pre-arranged time. The caller should try and concentrate on the receiver for a few minutes before making the call.

[4] When the phone rings, the receiver has to say who they think is calling before they pick it up.

[5] The receiver then accepts the call to find out if they were correct.

[6] Repeat the experiment as many times as possible with different groups of people, making sure to keep records of the number of right and wrong answers given.

[7] Take note that according to the law of chance, the receiver should pick the correct friend one in four times (25 percent of the time). According to Rupert Sheldrake, if the results are significantly higher this is statistically important and may indicate the involvement of telepathy.

Rupert Sheldrake

UPTON SINCLAIR

Upton Sinclair (1878–1968) was a Pulitzer Prize-winning American author who wrote more than 90 books in a variety of genres. Sinclair's book *Mental Radio*, published in 1930, with a preface by Albert Einstein, was an influential work in the field of the paranormal. For example, psychologist William McDougall (1871–1938) was influenced by the book to establish the parapsychology department at Duke University, headed by J. B. Rhine.

In *Mental Radio*, Sinclair describes a remarkable series of experiments with his second wife, Mary Craig Kimbrough, who was convinced she had telepathic abilities. In order to prove she had these powers, Sinclair devised a series of almost 300 tests which took place over a three year period (1928–1930). The results of these tests proved to him not only that telepathy was real, but that it could be tested and verified scientifically.

The usual procedure for the telepathy tests detailed in *Mental Radio* was for Sinclair to shut himself up in his study and draw a picture of anything that came into his head and place it in a sealed envelope (though after a while the couple abandoned going to the trouble of using envelopes). Meanwhile, in another room some distance away, "Craig," as his wife

Left **Psychologist William McDougall.**

was known, would attempt to "receive" the image and draw it. In all Craig produced 290 of these drawings, which included animals, trees, stars, household objects, hats or whatever came into Sinclair's mind. The results of these experiments, according to *Mental Radio*, were 65 (23 percent) successes, 155 (53 percent) partial successes, and 70 (24 percent) failures. Although the experiments were of course not conducted in a controlled scientific environment, their success rate seems to be far above that expected by chance. Sinclair believed the couple had discovered something important in their tests, what he referred to as a "universal mind-stuff."

Sinclair was not the first to carry out telepathy experiments with his wife. Previously, Craig would record a telepathic message sent from her brother, Robert Irwin, who lived in Pasadena, California, 40 miles (65km) away from the Sinclairs' house in Long Beach. For these tests, Craig and her brother would allocate a certain time each day, when Craig would lie on a couch in her study attempting to reach a trance state, while Robert would sketch some random object. On July 13, 1928, Craig received a mental image from her brother and noted down simply "Saw a table fork. Nothing else." Because of the distance, a few days passed before they were able to judge the success of the experiment. On July 15, Craig and Robert compared notes and it was revealed that he had drawn a picture of a table fork.

In 1932, Walter Franklin Prince, a research officer from the Boston based American Society for Psychical Research, carried out an independent analysis of Sinclair's results. In April of that year, Prince published a report of his findings in an appendix to the Society's sixteenth bulletin, where he stated that the data could not be explained in terms of fraud, chance, or educated guessing. The title of his article "The Sinclair Experiments Demonstrating Telepathy," show his positive opinion of Sinclair's tests. It must be noted that when the Sinclairs published their results in *Mental Radio*, they only discussed successful examples of their tests. Their failures were intentionally omitted, not only to make the book more interesting, but also because the couple were worried that the readers would be left with the impression that telepathy was not real.

Sinclair's telepathy experiment involved receiving images and drawing them.

SEE ALSO

Telepathy **Pages 27–33**
Extrasensory perception
Pages 16–21

CLAIRVOYANCE

lairvoyance is the ability to perceive objects, physical events, persons, or images not discernible using the ordinary sense channels. The word is derived from the French, *clair* meaning "clear," and *voyance* meaning "vision," so clairvoyance literally means the ability to have "clear vision." Part of the wider category of paranormal power known as extrasensory perception (ESP), clairvoyance can be experienced in a normal state, during meditation or trance, in sleep, while experiencing extreme stress, or in an altered state induced by hallucinogenic drugs, fasting, or illness.

Pearl Curran "channeling" the spirit of Patience Worth.

A number of the powers discussed in this book come under the heading of clairvoyance, including the ability to see into the past (retrocognition) or future (precognition); to determine the history of an object or its owner through touch (psychometry); to gather information about an object, place, or person through supernatural means (remote viewing); and to see events in the future, present, or past by means of a crystal ball, mirror, pool of water, or pendulum (scrying).

Clairvoyance is often popularly known as "second sight," the "sixth sense," or sometimes "prophetic sight" or "prophetic vision." The ability can be broken down into five types (see page 40–41): clairsentience (feeling/touching), clairaudience (hearing/listening), clairalience (smelling), claircognizance (knowing), and clairgustance (tasting). In New Age belief systems, clairvoyance describes a non-physical inner vision, an ability to see beyond the material world to the spiritual

reality which lies beyond. Skeptics contend that if clairvoyance were real it would have been proven by now, and regard it, and ESP, as pseudoscience.

Although the term "clairvoyance" did not appear in English until 1840, the phenomenon of second sight has a much longer history, from the "pythia" (seeress) at the Delphic oracle in ancient Greece, to seers of the Scottish Highlands in the seventeenth century, the medicine/holy men of Australian aboriginal and Native American tribes, and the mediums and psychics of the nineteenth, twentieth, and twenty-first centuries.

One of the best known clairvoyants of modern times was Jeane Dixon (1904–1997). Wisconsin-born Dixon,

There are reports of clairvoyance throughout history in most cultures.

who was known as "the clairvoyant to the stars," was hailed as a clairvoyant of exceptional perception and accuracy, who is said to have predicted the deaths of Hollywood actress Carole Lombard, the suicide of Marilyn Monroe, and the assassination of John F. Kennedy. Dixon was also "psychic advisor" to Richard Nixon and one of a number of astrologers who advised Nancy Reagan during Ronald Reagan's presidency (1981–1989).

However, skeptics point out that Dixon's numerous failed predictions, which include the beginning of World War III in 1958, that John F. Kennedy would not win the presidency in the 1960 election, that the Soviets would beat the US to the Moon, and that there

Above: A 1963 newspaper reporting the murder of president John F. Kennedy.

would be peace on earth by the year 2000, are rarely mentioned when her supporters laud her clairvoyant abilities.

Critics call this bias "the Jeane Dixon effect," a term introduced by John Allen Paulos, a mathematician at Temple University, Philadelphia. The "Jeane Dixon effect" is in essence the tendency of the mass media to hype a few correct predictions by a psychic while ignoring the much larger number of incorrect predictions. Even so, Dixon herself admitted that many of her predictions were failures, and insisted that clairvoyance is not an exact science and should therefore not be judged by strict scientific laws.

Above: President Richard Nixon referred to Jeane Dixon as "the soothsayer."

MAIN TYPES OF CLAIRVOYANCE

CLAIRSENTIENCE (FEELING/TOUCHING)

"Clear feeling": The power to touch an object or person and acquire knowledge from the "energy" surrounding that person or thing. The term is generally used to describe being able to psychically feel the "vibration" of other people. Clairsentience can apparently be used to pick up on the thoughts or emotions of other people, or even to detect illness.

CLAIRAUDIENCE (HEARING/LISTENING)

"Clear hearing": The ability to hear things, such as voices, music, and sounds, which are beyond the range of the ordinary power of hearing.

Clairaudience came to the fore during the spiritualist movement of the late nineteenth and early twentieth centuries when numerous mediums claimed to be guided by the voice of their individual spirit guide, with the voice sometimes speaking through the medium at séances. Clairaudience is considered a form of channeling, where the "sensitive" receive messages, often referred to as "cosmic" or "psychic vibrations," in thought form from another "frequency" or realm. The "entities" responsible for these voices are thought by psychics to inhabit a different world than humans, and may be deceased loved ones, spirit guides, angels, dark or negative forces, and in more recent times, aliens. The voices are not "heard" in the normal sense of the word, but are received on the "inner mental ear."

CLAIRALIENCE (SMELLING)

"Clear smelling": The ability to smell things that have no apparent physical source. Those people with the alleged power of clairalience can smell the odor associated with a person who has passed on from the earth plane, usually in the form of flowers, perfume, pipe or cigarette tobacco, or food smells. In some ghost stories a smell connected with a phantom often defines whether it is good or evil—a pleasant smell, usually of flowers, is associated with a friendly ghost, while a stale, rank odor is associated with an unpleasant or threatening ghost. These "olfactory ghosts" ultimately derive from medieval Christian biographies of saints, where angels and saints exuded sweet-smelling fragrances, while the Devil gave off a horrible sulfur-like odor.

CLAIRCOGNIZANCE (KNOWING)

"Clear knowing": Having knowledge of certain places, people, or situations without possessing the necessary information to know, i.e. without seeing, hearing, or feeling it. This inner knowledge can sometimes take the form of premonitions. Some psychics believe that a spirit guide or the "higher self" puts certain information into the receiver's mind, which often comes to them as a sudden flash of knowing, as fully-formed thoughts or insights into something they had no conscious knowledge of previously.

CLAIRGUSTANCE (TASTING)

"Clear tasting": Being aware of tastes without physically putting anything in the mouth. In other words, clairgustance is the ability to taste through your psychic rather than physical senses. A psychic may have the ability to detect a non-physical being through clairgustance, perhaps through a favorite food associated with the deceased entity.

HOW TO

TEST FOR CLAIRVOYANCE

1. HOW MANY PEOPLE ARE KNOWN TO HAVE HAD THIS POWER?

As with ESP, of which clairvoyance is a part, it is difficult to say, though there have been a number of well-known modern clairvoyants, including Jeane Dixon and Doris Stokes.

2. HOW IS THE POWER ACQUIRED?

Many find that this power lies latent in them until an unusual occurance brings the power to life.

3. HOW DO I KNOW IF I HAVE THE POTENTIAL TO DEVELOP THIS POWER?

You will have a feeling that you sense things around you more clearly than others do.

4. WHAT MATERIALS WILL I NEED FOR THE TESTS?

A table, paper, and pen for the "geographical locations" test.

5. WHAT ARE THE DANGERS ASSOCIATED WITH THIS POWER?

Over-use of this power can leave you feeling emotionally drained.

TEST 1
GEOGRAPHICAL LOCATIONS

This test requires 3 people.

[1] Make sure you and one other person are sitting comfortably, a few feet away from each other. You will need a small table in front of you.

[2] Note down 10 geographical locations on different pieces of paper.

[3] Choose one piece of paper, and concentrate hard on things that describe that location.

[4] Ask the other person to try and focus their mind and verbally describe the location they are seeing.

[5] The third person must record these impressions, no matter how strange or irrelevant they may seem.

[6] Take the next slip of paper and repeat the concentration process. Do this for all 10 locations, making sure you put the slips of paper down on the table in the order you took them out.

[7] Compare the locations written on the slips of paper with the records of your friend's impressions—how do they compare? Were there any hits?

[8] Repeat the exercise but change the roles of each person. Record whether this affects the success rate of the tests. Are certain people better at "sending" impressions than "receiving" them, for example?

TEST 2

ARE YOU CLAIRVOYANT?
A SIMPLE Q&A

	QUESTION	YES	NO
1	Have you ever seen what you thought was a ghost?		
2	Have you ever heard your name being called when you were sure you were alone?		
3	Do you ever feel that there is someone else in the room when you know you are alone?		
4	Have you ever smelled scents that have no discernible origin, e.g. flowers, strong perfume, cigarette/pipe smoke?		
5	Do you often have strong hunches about people/forthcoming events that ultimately prove to be correct?		
6	When the phone rings do you usually know who is calling before picking up the receiver (or looking at the screen on your cell phone)?		
7	When you are sitting with someone do impressions ever come into your mind which you believe may be the thoughts of the other person?		
8	Have you ever had the impression that another person is ill before they have found out themselves?		

If you answer "yes" to four or more of the above, you are probably clairvoyant.

APOLLONIUS OF TYANA

Apollonius of Tyana.

Apollonius was born in the first century in Tyana (modern Bor in southern Turkey), in what was then the Roman province of Cappadocia. According to popular accounts, mainly by his primary biographer, Philostratus the Elder (*c*.170–247 CE), Apollonius was a charismatic philosopher, teacher, vegetarian, miracle worker, prophet, and clairvoyant. He was also a contemporary of Jesus, with whom he has often been compared. During his lifetime and afterward, Apollonius achieved legendary fame, and his teachings have influenced both scientific and spiritual thought for more than two millennia.

One of the strangest tales concerning Apollonius is reported in Philostratus' *Life of Apollonius of Tyana*. The story involves the wedding of a young man called Menippus, a former student of Apollonius, who lived in the Greek city of Corinth. Menippus was about to marry a beautiful foreign woman, but while attending the wedding feast, Apollonius realized that something about the bride was not right. After studying the girl, he realized that she was in fact a Lamia (in Greek mythology, the beautiful queen of Libya who was transformed into a child-eating daemon) who planned to devour Menippus after the wedding.

> . . . you must regard this adornment, for it is not reality but the semblance of reality. And that you may realize the truth of what I say, this fine bride is one of the vampires, that is to say of those beings whom the many regard as lamias and hobgoblins. These beings fall in love, and they are devoted to the delights of Aphrodite, but especially to the flesh of human beings, and they decoy with such delights those whom they mean to devour in their feasts.

EXTRACT FROM PHILOSTRATUS' LIFE OF APOLLONIUS OF TYANA

APOLLONIUS OF TYANA

To prove his theory, Apollonius used his powers to make the luxurious banquet and its guests vanish, showing them to be a hallucination created by the girl, who turned back into her original Lamia form. This peculiar tale, illustrating Apollonius's philosophy of the dangers of a materialistic society, was the basis for the Romantic poet John Keats's 1819 poem "Lamia."

There are two ancient sources for what is surely one of the earliest cases of clairvoyance on record, Philostratus, and Roman historian Cassius Dio (*c.*150–235 CE), in his *Roman History*. On September 18, 96 CE, Roman emperor Domitian was murdered in Rome in a palace

Above **Tyana was an ancient city of Anatolia in Turkey.**

conspiracy organized by court officials, with a certain steward, Stephanus, striking the first blow with his dagger. According to the story, at the very moment of the assassination, Apollonius was delivering a speech many hundreds of miles away in the city of Ephesus (on the west coast of modern Turkey), when his voice suddenly dropped and he lost concentration. He then fell silent for a minute, glanced at the ground and then suddenly, in a voice very different from his own, cried out "Good, Stephanus! Bravo, Stephanus! Smite the bloodthirsty wretch! You

Left **Apollonius of Tyana reveals to Menippus of Corinth that his wife is an evil spirit, by demonstrating her true appearance.**
Right **A Roman mosaic from Pompeii depicting a "magical consultation."**

have struck, you have wounded, you have slain." There was another pause, and Apollonius finally said, "Take heart, gentlemen, for the tyrant has been slain this day."

We know that Apollonius was highly antagonistic to Domitian; the emperor's reign was said to be one of terror and persecution for philosophers. Apollonius thus regarded Domitian as a tyrant and considered his death to be a positive and happy event. Consequently, some researchers (rather than believing in Apollonius's supernatural powers regarding knowledge of the emperor's death)

have suggested that the sage may have been informed of the details of the plot to assassinate Domitian beforehand, or could even have been involved in its planning.

SEE ALSO

Extrasensory perception
Pages 17–21
Telepathy **Pages 27–33**

PRECOGNITION

Precognition (from the Latin *precognition*) means literally "prior or previous knowledge." In paranormal terms the word has come to mean the ability to obtain direct knowledge or a vision of a future event through extrasensory means. This faculty of "seeing the future" is also called "second sight." Premonitions (a "feeling" that something is going to happen) and also prophecy, are closely related powers to precognition. Of all types of extrasensory perception (ESP), precognition is the most reported, the majority of cases occurring in people's dreams. Precognition may also occur as momentary flashes of the future during the waking state, as auditory hallucinations, or may even be induced by trance.

Tragic events such as natural disasters are often claimed to have been foreseen by precognition.

Most cases of precognition occur a relatively short time before the future event, usually within twenty-four hours; on extremely rare occasions the experiences may take place weeks, months, or even years before the event takes place. Precognition often involves tragic events such as death, illness, accidents like airplane crashes, and natural disasters such as earthquakes. Many parapsychologists believe that precognition represents a glimpse of one of many possible futures, whose outcome is based on current conditions and existing information. Both of these latter factors may be changed by a person's free will. Other researchers believe that precognition demonstrates the disturbing fact that the future is immutable, it is already written in stone, and our free will is no more than an illusion.

Toward the end of the nineteenth century, the British Society for Psychical Research (SPR) collected and reviewed a number of cases of apparent precognition, but it was not until the first quarter of the twentieth century that the first systematic study of precognition was undertaken, by British aeronautics engineer John Williams Dunne (1875–1949). The results of this study were published in Dunne's 1927 book, *An Experiment with Time*.

Dunne's interest in precognition began one night in 1899, when he dreamt that his watch had stopped at half past four. He woke up and found that this had actually happened. This was the first of his many "precognitive dreams" which involved both mundane incidents in his own life and important national events appearing in newspapers the day following his dream. On one occasion in 1913, Dunne dreamt of a train crashing over a high railroad embankment he knew was close to the Forth Railway Bridge in Scotland. He "felt" that the incident occurred in March or April. On

April 14, 1914, the Flying Scotsman crashed just 15 miles (25km) north of the Forth Railway Bridge.

Dunne's research found that precognitive dreams were fairly common and he eventually worked out a complicated theory to explain them. In simple terms Dunne believed that life was similar to a roll of film going through a projector, but in dreams the mind has the ability to "jump forward" and glimpse what comes further on in the film. Although Dunne's ideas about the nature of time were rejected by the scientific community, *An Experiment with Time* has become something of a classic in the paranormal field.

The work of J.B. Rhine on ESP, (see pages 17–21) at Duke University, included much that was relevant to

> Precognition is the perception of future events through extrasensory means.

Dunne dreamt that a train would crash near Forth Railway Bridge.

the study of precognition. Impressed by *An Experiment with Time*, Rhine adapted his card-guessing test to investigate precognition by simply asking his subjects to guess the next card in the pack, rather than the one that was face down on the table.

Rather more controversial in the field of precognition is Samuel George Soal (1889–1975), a British mathematician and psychical researcher who carried out a series of precognition experiments from 1941–1943. The simple test devised by Soal and his colleagues was to ask the subject to identify which of five cards containing animal symbols a subject in another room was looking at. The results of Soal's experiments, with photographer Basil Shackleton, showed that the subject had scored an incredible 1,101 hits from 3,789 cards, well above the number allowed by chance. Parapsychologists hailed Soal's work as finally proving the existence of ESP, and J.B. Rhine, whose work and methods Soal had criticized severely, generously described Soal's experiments as "a milestone in the field." Though there were a few dissenting voices at the time, it was not until 1978 that the experiments were found to be fraudulent: Soal, it was discovered, had altered his data to create more hits.

The exposure of the Soal experiments leads us to the question of whether the evidence for precognition stands up to scientific scrutiny. Skeptics' biggest criticism of precognition is that in cases where people believe they have a gift for seeing future events, a process known as "selection bias" is at work. In other words people remember when their "visions" of the future were accurate but forget when they were

Left: Samual G. Soal destroyed his own reputation by falsifying the results of his tests.

completely wrong. Cryptomnesia has also been put forward as an explanation for cases of precognition. Cryptomnesia is when a person possesses facts about something that will occur in the future but loses conscious knowledge of how they obtained this information. When the event actually occurs they believe that they received knowledge of it without the help of normal channels of information. Scientists insist that in order to show that precognition is anything beyond a special class of coincidence, controlled demonstrations of the ability would have to be carried out on a regular basis. That no-one with the ability of "second sight" has ever volunteered themselves for such tests is enough to convince skeptics that the supernatural power of precognition is entirely exaggerated.

HOW TO

TEST FOR PRECOGNITION

1. HOW MANY PEOPLE ARE KNOWN TO HAVE HAD THIS POWER?

This is quite a commonly reported power, for many people experience what they believe to be precognitive dreams.

2. HOW IS THE POWER ACQUIRED?

Precognition is often hereditary, although it often manifests itself later in life, especially around the menopause for women.

3. WHAT ARE THE EARLY WARNING SIGNS?

Perhaps momentary precognitive visions or dreams.

4. HOW DO I KNOW IF I HAVE THE POTENTIAL TO DEVELOP THIS POWER?

If you have had feelings about future events that have repeatedly turned out to be true.

5. WHAT MATERIALS WILL I NEED FOR THE TEST?

An ordinary pack of playing cards, pen, and paper, for the playing card test.

6. WHAT ARE THE DANGERS ASSOCIATED WITH THIS POWER?

There are no obvious dangers associated with exercising precognition, although you may find yourself becoming overly focused on what might happen.

TEST

PLAYING CARD TEST

This simple precognition test requires two people; you will also need an ordinary pack of playing cards, a pen, and some paper.

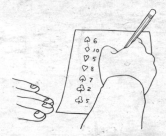

[3] Make yourself comfortable and try to clear your mind. Picture the playing cards in your mind's eye, and then write down on a sheet of paper the order in which you think the cards will occur, noting the card number and suit.

[1] Get another person to remove the four aces from the pack of playing cards.

[2] Ask them to shuffle the rest of the cards thoroughly.

[4] Ask the other person to turn the remaining 48 cards over one at a time, recording as they do so the number and suite of each card.

[5] The other person then compares your predicted order with the actual order of the cards as they occurred, and notes your score.

[6] Any score of four or more correct matches (there is only a 1 in 50 chance of doing this) suggests that something other than chance was at work—could it be precognition?

CASE STUDY

STELLA C.

The medium "Stella C." (Dorothy Stella Cranshaw) was born in 1900 in North Woolwich, UK, the daughter of a charcoal burner. During the 1920s she gave a series of sittings (or séances), organized by controversial psychical researcher Harry Price (1891–1948), at the National Laboratory of Psychical Research in London. It was at one of these sittings, on April 12, 1923, that the 22-year-old Stella C., then working as a nurse in a London hospital, exhibited an apparently clear case of precognition. During this particular sitting there had been much of the usual séance room phenomena, raps, unusual table movement, and communications from Stella C.'s "spirit guide" Palma.

About halfway through the séance, Stella C. fell into a semi-trance and stated to one of the sitters, a Miss Phillimore, that she could clearly see a newspaper—the front page of the *Daily Mail*, with the date "May 19, 1923." She added that she could also see the name "Andrew Salt" written in large letters. In addition, Stella C. also felt a "sensation" of seeing a boy falling, and a doctor bending over him, pouring out a white powder from a bottle or tin which he was giving the boy. At the time very little importance was attached to the vision. Then, thirty-seven days later, the *Daily Mail* appeared, and on its front page was a large advertisement for Andrews Liver Salts, featuring a picture of an upset boy who has spilled salt onto the floor from a plate he is holding.

Above **The medium, Stella C.**
Left **Psychical researcher, Harry Price.**

STELLA C.

Harry Price contacted the manufacturers of the salts who assured him that they had not shown the poster to anyone until May, and the *Daily Mail* stated that they had not received the picture until three weeks before the advertisement ran (April 28). An apparent case of precognition? Unfortunately Harry Price is known to have "enhanced" the results of his parapsychology experiments on more than one occasion, so further investigations into the exact circumstances of the sitting would have to be carried out before any useful conclusions could be drawn from Stella C.'s prediction.

Not all the predictions of psychics were as apparently successful as that of Stella C. Many of Edgar Cayce's prophecies were vague, to say the least, and others (thankfully) way off the mark. For example, Cayce predicted calamitous earth changes between 1958 and 1998; including Californian superquakes and the submersion of New York and Japan, plus a catastrophic pole shift in 1998. However it was not all gloom and doom, Cayce insisted that the few survivors of this latter disaster would enjoy a higher level of existence than before.

Cayce also predicted that Atlantis would begin to rise again in 1968 or 1969, in the area of Bimini, near the Bahamas. Indeed Cayce's supporters became extremely excited when in 1968–69 strange underwater structures were discovered exactly where Cayce had predicted. Zoologist Dr. Manson Valentine and underwater cinematographer Dimitri Rebikoff located and explored the "Bimini Road"—which consisted of long, regular walls of cyclopean blocks (some weighing more than 80 tons) in shallow water north-west of Bimini Island. However, in 1980,

Left **Edgar Cayce, an American psychic healer.**

Eugene Shinn of the US Geological Survey published the conclusions of his detailed examinations of the mysterious underwater stones. Shinn stated that his tests indicated that the stones must have been laid there by natural means, and the "Bimini Road" was soon forgotten.

Without doubt, the most famous instance of precognition involves the sinking of the great "unsinkable" liner, the *Titanic*, in April 1912. William Thomas Stead's prophetic 1892 fictional article about the sinking of a huge liner in the North Atlantic is discussed in another chapter (see Automatic Writing, page 97), but Stead was not the only one

Left **The Sinking of the Titanic, 1912, a painting by Willy Stöewer.**

speed was twenty-three knots), it was equipped with only twenty-four lifeboats (the *Titanic* had twenty), the *Titan* was 800 feet (240m) in length (the *Titanic* was 882½ feet/270m), and it had a passenger capacity of 3,000 (the same as the *Titanic*). Both the *Titan* and the *Titanic* had three propellers and two masts.

Many people believe that the only explanation for these uncanny similarities is that the author Morgan Robertson had somehow seen a prophetic vision of the ill-fated *Titanic*. Skeptics argue, however, that another explanation is possible. The names, critics insist, could easily have been coincidental; after all, classical mythology was extremely popular at the end of the nineteenth century, so the name Titan (one of a race of giant pre-Olympian Greek gods) would be entirely natural for a huge, powerful ocean liner. The author of *Futility*, Morgan Robertson, also had a considerable knowledge of ships, having been to sea as a cabin boy, and later spending ten years as a merchant seaman. It is also a fact

that in the early twentieth century, collisions between ships and icebergs in the North Atlantic were fairly common, especially during spring, when icebergs drifted south. Nevertheless, the list of coincidences between the sinking of the *Titanic* and the story of the *Titan* is a long one, and in the minds of many believers it remains an obvious case of precognition.

who appears to have had a premonition of the disaster.

In 1898 Morgan Robertson published a novel called *Futility*. In this work of fiction a great "unsinkable" liner hits an iceberg in the North Atlantic during April and sinks with huge loss of life. The name of the ship in Robertson's novel is the *Titan*. The more one looks into the details of the *Titan* the more startling the similarities become. Like the *Titanic*, the *Titan* was believed to be unsinkable due to its water-tight compartments. When the disaster occurred, the *Titan* was traveling at a speed of twenty-five knots (the *Titanic's*

SEE ALSO
- - - - - - - - - - - - - - - -
Automatic writing
Pages 97–102
Precognition **Pages 49–54**

RETROCOGNITION

he term "retrocognition" (also known as postcognition), describes the perception of a past scene or event which could not have been learned or inferred by normal means, such as from books or movies. The term was coined by Frederic William Henry Myers (1842–1901), founder member of the Society for Psychical Research. Retrocognition is closely related to the so-called "time slip," a phenomenon where a person or persons witnesses scenes or objects apparently from another time period (most usually the past).

In his book, *Haunted Britain* (1948), Elliot O'Donnell relates a fascinating retrocognition or "time slip" story. This tale involved a lady and her friend who were vacationing in the town of Chagford, on the north eastern edge of Dartmoor, an area of bleak moorland in southwest England.

One summer afternoon the two ladies decided to go for a walk on the moor, and after rambling around for a few hours they arrived at two picturesque cottages. The cottages made such an impression on the pair that they knocked on the door of one of them to inquire if there were any apartments available to rent. The door was answered by a pretty little fair-haired girl who asked them in to wait while she went to get her mother. While waiting inside the cottage, the two women noticed the curiously old-fashioned decoration and also an

F.W.H. Myers, philosopher, writer, and psychical researcher.

Could the women from 1951 have heard the terrifying war sounds of Dieppe in 1942?

Another tale concerns a purely auditory experience. Some time in 1951, two English women were on vacation near Dieppe when, early one morning, they both heard the sounds of cries, shouts, and gunfire. After a while the noise stopped, but soon started up again, and this time the two women were able to identify what they believed to be the distinctive sounds of dive bombers. Subsequent investigations of the case apparently discovered that the times the ladies reported the noises corresponded closely to those of battles during the invasion of Dieppe in 1942. Despite the loudness of the sounds, nobody else in the building had heard them, and without independent confirmation one wonders how objective the sounds were. One explanation put forward for this case of auditory retrocognition was that the women may have mistaken the sounds of a dredger working nearby at the time for the noises of a Second World War battle.

One extremely controversial retrocognition case was shown on the UK television show *Strange But True* in 1979. In October, 1979, two English couples, the Simpsons and the Gisbys, had gone on a driving trip together through France and Spain. The couples claimed that during the vacation they had stayed overnight at a peculiarly old-fashioned small hotel in the Rhone Valley near Montelimar, in southern France. The little hotel appeared to possess no modern conveniences such as telephones, televisions, or elevators, and instead of locks on the doors there were wooden latches. There were no pillows on the beds and there was no glass in the windows, only wooden shutters. The staff of the hotel and some local *gendarmes* the couple met there also seemed to be wearing very old-fashioned clothes. The next day, when the couples came to pay their bill they were astonished to find that they were charged only a few francs for the night's lodgings and the meals they had eaten.

Two weeks later, on their way back from traveling in Spain, the couples decided to drop in at the strange little hotel again, but although they took exactly the same route as before they were unable to locate it. A further surprise was to await the Simpsons and the Gisbys on

odd-looking black bird in a cage. When the girl's mother arrived, a tall, darkly attractive woman with a strange far-away look in her eyes, she told them that there was presently no room available in the cottages and so they left. The ladies were not to return to the area until the following year, when they decided to look for the cottages again. However, despite a thorough search they were unable to locate the buildings, though they did find the spot in which they thought the cottages had stood. Upon further enquiry, the two ladies discovered that no such cottages had ever existed in the area. Had the two ladies experienced retrocognition or were the cottage and its strange inhabitants themselves ghosts from the past?

their return to England. When they had their rolls of film from the vacation developed, the couples discovered that the pictures taken at the hotel had disappeared. This is a bizarre case, and although somewhat fascinating, remains suspicious. It is difficult to imagine that the manager of the time-traveling hotel, as well as the staff and the *gendarmes*, with whom the couples claimed they had interacted, would have displayed no reaction to such a "futuristic" mode of transportation as a modern car, or to their 1970s French currency.

In the 1990s there were various accounts of apparent retrocognition attached to a single street, Bold Street, in the center of Liverpool. A number of witnesses, including an off-duty police officer, reported being transported back in time while traveling along this road, finding themselves on a cobbled street with old-fashioned stores and people dressed in 1940s clothing.

Gardner Murphy, an American psychologist and psychical researcher.

These examples show us that retrocognition generally occurs spontaneously during normal daily life, though there are records of instances in dreams and by psychics during parapsychology experiments. The experience of retrocognition usually takes the form of a vision (skeptics would say an hallucination), where the modern "real" world disappears and is momentarily replaced by buildings, landscapes, and sometimes people from the past. Sometimes (as in the Versailles case, see page 64) the onset of precognition is immediately preceded by a sense of physical and mental oppression. There is an insightful theory, put forward by American psychologist Gardner Murphy (1890–1975), among others, that the majority of ghostly apparitions are in fact cases of retrocognition. According to this theory, a person experiencing retrocognition becomes momentarily displaced in time and is able to observe scenes from the past as they are happening. Intriguingly, this suggests that if people experiencing retrocognition are seen by past generations, they may be perceived as ghosts from the future.

Scientifically, of course, retrocognition is an untestable phenomenon, as there is no way of knowing whether the individual is experiencing anything objective at all. Aside from delusion and hallucination, a number of explanations have been put forward to explain retrocognition and time slips. Perhaps the witnesses were transported back in time, or were fortunately present when some kind of window on the past opened up allowing the observer to see through it. However, while interesting, such physics-defying explanations do not really clarify anything. They are unproven and entirely speculative theories which complicate the mystery rather than adding anything to our understanding of it. The majority of the evidence for retrocognition suggests that only certain types of people experience the phenomenon. Eleanor Jourdain, for example, seems to have been particularly prone to such "visions" (see page 64). If this is the case, then retrocognition may occur not in physical reality, but entirely within the mind of individuals who are easily impressed by certain external stimuli, which bring about a sudden change in their consciousness.

HOW TO

TEST FOR RETROCOGNITION

1. HOW MANY PEOPLE ARE KNOWN TO HAVE HAD THIS POWER?

This ability is extremely rare, with only a few known, recorded cases.

2. HOW IS THE POWER ACQUIRED?

The power seems to appear randomly without warning.

8. WHAT ARE THE EARLY WARNING SIGNS?

There are usually none, though occasionally if a person exhibits other "psychic abilities," this may suggest the capacity to experience retrocognition.

4. HOW DO I KNOW IF I HAVE THE POTENTIAL TO DEVELOP THIS POWER?

Perhaps you have experienced unexplained dreams of real past events of which you had no previous knowledge.

5. WHAT MATERIALS WILL I NEED FOR THE TEST?

Just your imagination.

6. WHAT ARE THE DANGERS ASSOCIATED WITH THIS POWER?

There are no obvious dangers.

TEST

KEEP A DREAM JOURNAL

Retrocognition is almost impossible to test, though traces of events from the distant past may emerge in dreams.

One way to check this is to keep a dream journal.

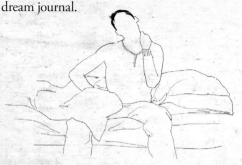

[3] At the end of the period read carefully through your dairy entries. Do certain people, places, or events from the past keep cropping up? Did you see yourself in your dream? Make a note of all the details.

[1] As soon as you wake up in the morning (or during the night) and you are conscious of having had a dream, write down as much as you can remember, not leaving out any details no matter how trivial.

[2] Continue to record in your journal for a certain period of time (a week, to over a month).

[4] When you have enough material from you diaries, do some historical research and try and identify which period you have been dreaming of. Can you identify people and events in history from your journal notes? Did you receive knowledge from your dreams about these events which you could not have known from any other source? If the answer is yes, then perhaps you experienced a form of retrocognition.

A dream journal is a diary in which dream experiences are recorded. Psychologists have demonstrated that each of us dreams every night, but most of these dreams are quickly forgotten. Thus, keeping a dream journal helps you retain the information for longer. Indeed the very act of recording a dream in this way over a period of time can have the effect of improving your ability to recall dreams, and can help you identify any recurring themes running through them.

Many psychics believe that the dream journal is one of the most helpful tools in dream interpretation as it allows the individual not only to understand their dreams but also to access their own inner knowledge. Although, traditionally, people have recorded their dreams in notebook journals, or sometimes using audio recording devices, nowadays more people are turning to the internet where they can create digital dream journals online.

VERSAILLES TIME SLIP

The most celebrated and controversial retrocognition experience is unquestionably that of Charlotte Moberley (1846–1937) and Eleanor Jourdain (1863–1924), the principal and vice-principal of St Hugh's College, Oxford (UK). One August afternoon in 1901, the two academics were visiting the Palace at Versailles, now located in a suburb of Paris, and decided to go and search the grounds of the palace for Marie Antoinette's small private château, the Petite Trianon.

While wandering around the grounds, both ladies claimed they felt a strange sense of oppression in the atmosphere, and encountered a number of people dressed in late eighteenth-century clothes, as well as landscape and architecture which they later believed to have been present in the park in 1789 (the year that the mobs of the French Revolution stormed Versailles), rather than the beginning of the twentieth century. The two ladies' subsequent research into the period of the French Revolution persuaded them that they had somehow caught a glimpse of the year 1789 and met with members of the court of Louis XVI and Marie Antoinette (1755–1793), as well as encountered the legendary French queen herself. Moberley and Jourdain did not publish their experience until 1911, in the form of a book called *An Adventure*, under the pseudonyms Elizabeth Morison and Frances Lamont. Ever since the publication of *An Adventure* there has been

Left **Charlotte Moberley**

Above **Eleanor Jourdain**

heated debate about the strange experience at Versailles, based substantially on the question of how the ladies could have learned the details of the layout of the palace and grounds of Versailles in the year of 1789 without prior knowledge of the history of the area.

One prosaic explanation for what the English ladies saw was suggested by French author Philippe Jullian, in his 1965 book, *Prince of Aesthetes: Count Robert De Montesquiou 1855–1921*. Jullian wrote that in their wanderings around Versailles, Moberley and Jourdain had probably encountered French aristocrat and poet, Marie Joseph Robert Anatole, Comte de Montesquiou-Fezenzac, who was living at Versailles around the time of their visit. Montesquiou on occasion held fancy dress parties in the grounds of the palace, where he and his friends would dress in

period costumes and perform *tableaux vivants* ("living pictures"), re-enacting paintings, sculptures, and historical scenes. Could such parties involving the French decadent avant-garde of the period answer the descriptions given by the two English ladies? Perhaps, though tempting as it is to accept Jullian's explanation for what the two ladies experienced, it still leaves the matter of the different scenery they claimed to have seen unaccounted for. It has also never been shown beyond question that Montesquiou and his friends were at Versailles the same day on which Moberley and Jourdain were visiting.

Critics of the Versailles case, including W.H. Salter of the Society for Psychical Research, have noted that a large amount of the material relating to Moberley and Jourdain's "time slip" experience, which they supposedly recorded in 1901, was in fact written down much later, in 1906— after they had researched the history of Versailles. This is an important point, as the ladies were supposedly ignorant of the details of French-Revolution-period Versailles in 1901, and so would not have been able to give accurate descriptions of it.

In a 1911 review of *An Adventure*, another leading member of the British Society for Psychical Research, Eleanor Sidgwick, dismissed the book as nothing more than a product of mutual confabulation. Although it certainly seems unlikely that two respected academics would have invented the story, it is possible that while walking around the grounds of Versailles, perhaps suffering from overtiredness and being lost, historical events which they had read or heard about produced a "bygone Versailles" in their mind's eye. Of much importance when considering the Versailles case is that Eleanor Jourdain also claimed to have had numerous "psychic visions" of scenes from the past in Oxford in 1902. Whatever the

The ladies experienced a time slip in the gardens of the Palace of Versailles.

explanation, as long as they lived the two women sincerely believed they had experienced something uncanny on their visit to Versailles in 1901.

SEE ALSO

Retrocognition **Pages 59–63**
Clairvoyance **Pages 37–44**

PSYCHIC MEDIUMSHIP

It is the spiritualist belief that human personality survives bodily death and lives on in another form. The term "medium" (or sometimes "sensitive") is applied to those people who function as intermediaries between the living and the "spirits of the dead" during séances. There are two types of mediumship: "mental" and "physical." Mental mediums use their minds and bodies as channels (hence the term "channeling") through which the spirits of the dead can communicate. Physical mediums produce physical "paranormal" phenomena, such as loud raps, voices, psychokinesis, and materialized spirit bodies. The source of power for such manifestations is thought to be the medium themselves, who uses their "spiritual energy," or in the Victorian era, the strange substance known as "ectoplasm," to produce séance phenomena.

The practice of communicating with the spirit world using an intermediary is an ancient one. The priestess or pythia, as she was known, who went into a trance to make prophecies at the ancient Greek oracle of Delphi (at its peak between the sixth and fourth centuries BC), is an early example. The Old Testament account of the Witch of Endor relates the story of the raising of the spirit of the prophet Samuel so the Hebrew king Saul is able to question him regarding an approaching battle.

The heyday of mediumship coincided for the most part with the spread of spiritualism in the US and Europe during the mid-to-late nineteenth century. Of the thousands practicing the art, or more often than

An engraving of Saul and the Witch of Endor.

not, the deception of mediumship, only one or two stand out as notable and unusual individuals. One of these is Daniel Dunglas Home (1833–1886), a Scottish-born medium who displayed an apparently startling array of strange talents including levitation, psychokinesis, and the playing of remote musical instruments. Controversial, (she was caught cheating on a number of occasions), Italian medium Eusapia Palladino (1854–1918) is alleged to have sent heavy tables and sofas flying into the air, caused sudden drops in temperature, materialized human-like limbs and

Left: Home conducted hundreds of séances, attended by some of the most well-known names of the Victorian period.

SÉANCE ROOM PHENOMENA

Traditional séances, especially during the late nineteenth and early twentieth centuries, were held in a darkened room, though modern séances are occasionally held in normal light. Generally at a séance, the "sitters" will be sat around a table, usually holding hands, and will sometimes be encouraged to sing, or perhaps relaxing music will be played. The music and the dim lighting conditions are supposed to encourage the spirits to make contact, though skeptics argue that they create an ideal opportunity for fraud. The medium, usually a woman, then goes into a trance, and her "spirit" guide communicates

through her. During "materialization" séances, a wide range of bizarre phenomena have been witnessed by observers.

TABLE-RAPPING
Loud knocks on the table, or from elsewhere in the room were said to be the spirits trying to communicate.

TABLE TILTING
The séance table moves of its own accord, despite being held down by the sitters, levitating upward or even crashing around the room.

LEVITATION
Objects in the room, such as tables, pianos, and chairs levitate.

COLD BREEZES
Cold breezes or noticeable drops in temperature have been recorded at séances.

attracted distant objects toward her. The story of Florence Cook (see page 73), allegedly the first British medium to produce full form materializations in front of witnesses, and her "spirit control" Katie King, is one that remains controversial to this day, and though most likely a fraud, she still remains worthy of further study.

Indeed it was the exposure of physical mediums, for example the Davenport Brothers and the Bangs Sisters in the US, using magic tricks to produce their physical phenomena, that caused mediumship to fall into disrepute. As the twentieth century progressed,

Right: A séance with Eusapia Palladino at the home of Camille Flammarion, 1898.

GHOSTLY MUSIC

Musical instruments in the room are played by invisible hands.

DISEMBODIED VOICES

Ghostly whispers or voices are heard.

LUMINOUS PHENOMENA

The appearance of lights or other luminous objects without apparent origin in the séance room.

APPORTS

The sudden appearance of small portable objects, known as "apports," in the séance room, through an apparent penetration of matter. Apports are usually flowers, though occasionally personal

possessions of the sitters such as a ring or an initialed handkerchief have been recorded.

ECTOPLASM

Term coined by parapsychologist Charles Richet (1850–1935) to describe the mysterious, grayish viscous substance which emanated apparently from the bodies of some physical mediums. Occasionally

this ectoplasm would form into the shape of human limbs or even fully formed spirit entities that walked freely among the sitters at the séance.

PHYSICAL MATERIALIZATIONS

The appearance of materialized spirit bodies or body parts such as heads, hands, and arms. These "spirits" would sometimes be formed from ectoplasm.

psychical mediumship became less practiced and most of the spectacular psychic phenomena associated with Victorian era paranormal "stars" like Home and Palladino disappeared. That is not to say that there have not been flamboyant, not to mention controversial, modern figures claiming to be in contact with spirits of the dead. Throughout the 1970s and 1980s, London-born Doris Stokes (1920–1987) "communicated with the dead" in front of huge stage and television audiences, and was the first medium to appear at the prestigious London Palladium, tickets selling out in only two hours.

American psychic, spiritual medium, and author, Sylvia Browne (born 1936), has been involved in high

Above: Doris Stokes helped to raise the profile of the psychic phenomena in the 1980s.

Above: The Davenport Brothers were American magicians in the late 1800s.

profile court cases and various controversies regarding her claims to have helped the police in missing person and murder cases and her failed predictions.

In general, however, the modern medium and the modern séance are rather less theatrical than during the golden age of spiritualism. For example, at the London headquarters of The Spiritualist Association of Great Britain, founded in 1872, those wishing to consult a medium are required to book an appointment with one of the resident "sensitives." The Spiritualist Association also offers "Hypnotherapy and Past Life Regression: By appointment only."

HOW TO

TEST FOR MEDIUMSHIP

1. HOW MANY PEOPLE ARE KNOWN TO HAVE HAD THIS POWER?

Hundreds, if not thousands, during the heyday of spiritualism in the late nineteenth century. Nowadays it is less common.

2. HOW IS THE POWER ACQUIRED?

Most mediums have said that it was a natural gift they have always had.

3. WHAT ARE THE EARLY WARNING SIGNS?

Perhaps poltergeist activity in the home of the prospective medium, or the person might sometimes exhibit mild PK or other "psychic abilities."

4. HOW DO I KNOW IF I HAVE THE POTENTIAL TO DEVELOP THIS POWER?

Unexplained movement of objects in your vicinity, or you may feel somehow able to communicate with those who have passed on.

5. WHAT MATERIALS WILL I NEED FOR THE TEST?

A large amount of focus and concentration.

6. WHAT ARE THE DANGERS ASSOCIATED WITH THIS POWER?

Exhaustion due to intense mental activity. Remember to focus afterward on yourself—it's important to retain your own mental and spiritual balance.

TEST

THE SITTER TEST

[1] Ask a friend to find a volunteer who will come and "sit" for you. It is essential that this person is unknown to you and you do not communicate with them in any way beforehand.

[2] It is also important that this person has something unique about them. It could be their job, a hobby, a specific tattoo on their body, or something that has recently happened to them. Your friend must write this down.

[3] The sitter must be in a chair opposite to you. Your friend should also be in the room with pen and paper ready to make notes.

[4] Relax and concentrate on the sitter for a few minutes and try and read what it is about them that is so unique.

[5] Don't rush yourself, when you are ready (when images or words related to this person come into your mind) say out loud what you think the unique thing is or which images or even random words you think may relate to their unique aspect.

[6] Allow yourself a few minutes to do this, then when you are ready, stop and check your friend's notes against what the person's unique characteristic was. How accurate were you? Do you have mediumistic abilities?

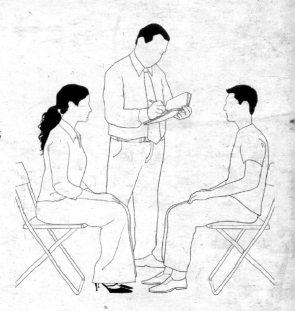

SPIRIT CABINETS

Spirit cabinets were introduced by mediums during the heyday of Spiritualism as part of the paraphernalia of the physical séance. The cabinet was a wooden or curtained closet which functioned both as the physical medium's work space and to section off the medium from the audience. Inside the closet the medium was often bound hand and foot, while seemingly incredible phenomena occurred around them.

FLORENCE COOK

The story of nineteenth-century physical medium Florence Cook and her "spirit control" Katie King is a controversial one. Allegedly the possessor of psychic abilities from a young age, Cook was to become famous in Victorian spiritualist circles and beyond for producing the full materialization of the spirit Katie King in front of numerous witnesses, and for undergoing methodical testing of her alleged psychic abilities by the eminent scientist Sir William Crookes. However, the genuineness of Cook's mediumistic abilities and the objectivity of Crookes investigations have been called into question by researchers who view the behavior of both the medium and the scientist as highly questionable.

Born on June 3, 1856, Florence Cook came from a respectable working-class home in Hackney, east London. After the age of fourteen, Cook began going into trances in front of the family and soon began to develop her own peculiar psychic gift, initially at informal séances held in the family house and in the house of a friend.

Soon Cook was giving impressive séances for a nearby spiritualist group called the Dalston Association of Enquirers into Spiritualism. It was at one of these séances, in the summer of 1872, that the floating spirit face of Katie King first appeared. The "entity" or "spirit" known as "Katie King" was somewhat of a spiritual world celebrity, first making herself known at the very beginnings of American Spiritualism in the early 1850s, at séances with mediums such as the Davenport Brothers and the Koons family, among others. Katie was allegedly the spirit of Annie Owen Morgan, the daughter of an historical seventeenth-century Welsh pirate called Henry Owen Morgan (1635–1688), known in the spirit world as John King. In her earthly incarnation she had apparently died young, around 22 or 23 years old, after committing a series of crimes which included murder. She had, she claimed, returned to convince the world of the truth of spiritualism in an attempt to expiate her earthly sins.

There are eyewitness accounts of varying reliability of what happened at Florence Cook's séances. Generally, after the medium was positioned inside her spirit cabinet (see page 72), the sitters would wait, occasionally for as long as 30 or 40 minutes, for the appearance of Katie, ashen faced and clad in flowing white robes, from behind the curtain. She would walk freely among the sitters, even allowing them to touch her, as the medium Florence apparently lay unconscious in the cabinet.

FLORENCE COOK

As word of Florence's physical mediumship spread she received the patronage of a Manchester businessman called Charles Blackburn. As Florence apparently never charged a fee for giving her séances she was glad of Blackburn's financial backing, which allowed her to demonstrate her mediumship whenever required.

However, on the night of December 9, 1873, her reputation as a physical medium received a blow from which it never fully recovered. One of the sitters at this particular session was a spiritualist and investigator named William Volckman. According to Volckman, after he had carefully observed the spirit of Katie King, dressed completely in ghostly white parading around the room, he became suspicious of the startling resemblance between the medium and the so-called spirit. Determined to prove his theory correct in dramatic fashion, Volckman sprang up from his chair and "grasped the spirit." In the confusion which followed, three of the other sitters took hold of Volckman, who received a scratched nose and lost part of his beard in the struggle, while the "spirit" escaped back into the cabinet.

When everything had calmed down, the curtain was pulled back. There the sitters found Florence in a considerably agitated condition, but still clad in the black dress and boots which she had been wearing at the beginning of the séance, and bound to the chair with the same tape which had been used to confine her. The knot in the tape, which had been sealed with the signet ring of the Earl of Caithness, one of the sitters, was still intact. A subsequent search of Florence Cook revealed no trace of the white robes which Katie King had been seen wearing. The thoroughness of this search is, however, not mentioned.

One of the most illustrious scientists to investigate the phenomenon of spiritualism was William (later Sir William) Crookes (1832–1919), an English chemist and physicist, and discoverer of the element thallium. Crookes held a series of test sittings with Florence Cook at his own house in Mornington Road, London, where he could be in complete control of the situation. Florence often stayed at the house, where Crookes lived with his wife Ellen, and was sometimes accompanied by her mother and sister Kate. In these experiments Crookes claimed to have witnessed the medium and the spirit together on more than one occasion, though critics have argued that when both Florence and Katie King were witnessed together, the medium must have had a collaborator, probably her sister Kate, to accomplish the deception.

During May 1874, as a visual record of his experiments with Florence Cook, Crookes took a series of 44 "spirit" photographs by artificial light using five different cameras. He described some of these photographs as "excellent." Unfortunately the handful of photographs of Katie King and Florence Cook that survive today look extremely unconvincing. Due to the resemblance between medium and spirit on these ghostly photographs, they are not taken seriously by psychical researchers

Florence Cook in a trance, with a spirit form behind her, during a séance at the home of Sir William Crookes.

today. Indeed these spirit photos have been enough to convince many researchers that Florence Cook and Katie King were indeed the same person, and that the whole thing was a fraud.

Shortly after these photographs were taken, Katie King ceased to appear at Cook's séances. However, despite the loss of her "spirit," Florence Cook continued her controversial career as a medium with varying degrees of success. On one occasion in January 1880, she was caught out apparently impersonating "Marie," her spirit guide; though some believed that she may have been "sleepwalking" at the time. The opinion of most researchers into the Florence Cook case is that Crookes and other investigators, as well as the sitters at her séances, were being hoodwinked by a clever illusionist. In fact this case could be held up as a classic example of the spiritualist phenomenon of the period, when the desire to believe in life after death was so strong that the critical facility of even the most scientific of investigators deserted them.

SEE ALSO

Extrasensory Perception
Pages 17–21
Channeling **Pages 77–81**

CHANNELING

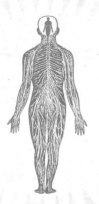

C hanneling is a New Age term used to describe a separate intelligence, whether disembodied spirits or sometimes even extraterrestrial beings, entering the body of the channeler and using their body and mind to directly communicate messages or prophecies. In the US, the term channeler has practically replaced the word medium to describe such a person. In some cases the channeler will, like mediums before them, go into a full trance, allowing the "entity" to take complete control of their body. In these cases the channeler allows the spirit to take possession of their mind and body, with the spirit talking through them, often in a very different voice than the channeler's own. The US channeler J.Z. Knight is an example of this. Other channelers maintain that they receive messages from their spirit guide through telepathy, that is, directly into their minds.

The current preoccupation with channeling, especially in the US, can be traced back to 1972 and the publication of the book, *Seth Speaks: The Eternal Validity of the Soul* by Jane Roberts and Robert F. Butts. Jane Roberts (1929–1984) was a New York born author, poet, and psychic, who in late 1963 had an experience which was to change her life forever. While Roberts and her husband Robert F. Butts were experimenting with an Ouija board, they began to receive communications from a deceased English teacher initially calling himself Frank Withers, though he later advised Roberts that he preferred to be known as "Seth."

Ouija board, also known as a "spirit board" or "talking board" is used to communicate with spirits.

An anonymous French civil servant, pictured above, claimed to have invented the Ouija board as early as 1908.

Before long, Roberts had discarded the Ouija board, instead going into a trance state where Seth would possess her body and speak through her. Roberts' husband would keep a record of Seth's mystical utterings. Seth informed Roberts that he was a non-physical being who had lived a number of lives on earth (one of which was, naturally, on Atlantis) to educate himself about the human condition. Seth's messages, which consisted mostly of monologs on a wide variety of New Age topics, including the boundless scope of the human consciousness, were eventually collected together and published as *The Seth Material*. The series of "Seth books" totaled ten volumes, and their publication established Roberts as one of the best known authors in the paranormal field. The manuscripts, notes, and recordings of *The Seth Material* were eventually donated by Roberts and Butts to Yale Library.

Although the most famous channeler, Roberts is not alone. J.Z. Knight (Judy Zebra Knight), was born Judith Darlene Hampton on March 16, 1946, in Roswell, New Mexico. In 1977, Knight was apparently visited by an entity named Ramtha, who informed her that he was the spirit of a 35,000-year-old warrior from the lost continent of Lemuria. Ramtha also told Knight that he had been betrayed and killed while leading a vast army of 2.5 million Lemurians against the Atlanteans. For the next two years Ramtha was Knight's personal tutor and spirit guide and has been passing on his wisdom and prophecies to the world through Knight.

Bizarre as the claims of J.Z. Knight are, Ramtha has amassed hoards of followers, including Hollywood legend Shirley MacLaine and *Dynasty* star Linda Evans. Knight has become hugely wealthy from her channeling, partly through her weekend seminars, for which she charges anything from US$400–$1,000 per person. During these seminars Ramtha passes on his teachings, which appear to be a hotchpotch of Jungian philosophy, Buddhist, Hindu, and Christian teachings, speaking in a suspiciously Hollywood version of Old English. The six-times married Knight is currently the president of JZK Inc and runs Ramtha's School of Enlightenment, located in the foothills of Mt. Rainier in Washington. The name of Ramtha is now copyrighted under J.Z. Knight.

As is to be expected, the attitude of the scientific community toward channeling is one of complete skepticism. Critics of the material channeled from spirit entities have the same objections as those critical of the spirit contacts of mediums during the late nineteenth century, namely the absolute banality of most of the channeled material. The "entities" present in cases like that of Jane Roberts and J.Z. Knight, skeptics argue, if not invented by the channelers for financial gain, are likely to be split-off elements of their own personalities. In their opinion, the creation of such "spirit guides" can be interpreted in the same light as multiple personality cases rather than the influence of any supernatural agency.

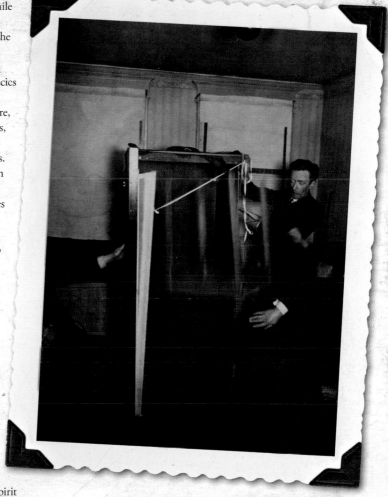

While attending a séance in the 1930s, Mrs. Poole of Winnipeg witnessed this allegedly paranormal levitation of a table.

HOW TO

TEST FOR CHANNELING

1. HOW MANY PEOPLE ARE KNOWN TO HAVE HAD THIS POWER?

As with mediums, there were a large number during the heyday of spiritualism in the late nineteenth century. Nowadays there are many claimed New Age channelers in the U.S. like J.Z. Knight, for example.

2. HOW IS THE POWER ACQUIRED?

Some claim to have received the gift from discarnate entities, others claim to have had it since birth.

3. WHAT ARE THE EARLY WARNING SIGNS?

A feeling that "someone" is trying to communicate through you.

4. HOW DO I KNOW IF I HAVE THE POTENTIAL TO DEVELOP THIS POWER?

Look for productive results with a Ouija board or the appearance of "psychic" abilities you didn't know you possessed.

5. WHAT MATERIALS WILL I NEED FOR THE TEST?

None.

6. WHAT ARE THE DANGERS ASSOCIATED WITH THIS POWER?

Mental exhaustion can lead to physical fatigue.

TEST

PRACTICE MEDITATING

Although there is no obvious way to test alleged communication with spirit beings, psychics claim that the key to successful channeling is to get yourself into a meditative state. The following is a simple way of doing this.

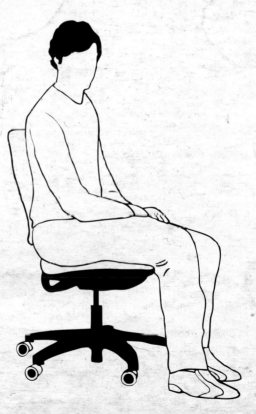

[1] Find or create a quiet, relaxing environment. Turn off the television, computer, radio, or stereo. If you must have music, make sure it is calm and relaxing.

[2] Sit in a comfortable chair, with your back in an upright position and your arms rested on your thighs. Make sure you're not so comfortable that you drift off to sleep.

[3] Consciously relax your whole body, beginning with your arms and legs.

[4] Focus your attention on your breathing and try to take slow, deep, rhythmic breaths.

[5] Silence your mind by clearing out all mental noise. Focus on emptying your mind completely until there is only silence.

[6] At this stage you can simply relax and benefit from the silence, or introduce an intention (for example to have a more positive outlook on life) and meditate on this desire.

[7] Try and find some time in your daily routine to meditate—even just for 5–10 minutes. The important thing is that meditation becomes a natural part of your daily life.

DOROTHY LOUISE EADY

Dorothy Louise Eady was born in a suburb of London in January 1904. According to Eady's own account, at the age of three she fell down a long flight of stairs and was pronounced dead by the attending doctor. However, an hour later the little girl was sitting up in bed, completely recovered. It was from this point onward that she began to have recurring dreams of being in an ancient building with huge columns, which she thought was a temple. When she was four years old her parents took her with them on a visit to the British Museum, where in the Egyptian galleries, the little girl suddenly realized she was "home." This realization was so strong that the little girl ran madly through the halls, kissing the feet of the ancient statues and eventually sitting down at the feet of a glass-cased mummy and refusing to budge.

Three years later Eady saw a photograph in a magazine showing the Temple of Sety the First at Abydos, and realized immediately that it was the large-columned building of her recurring dream. She informed her father that the temple was her home, the place where she had once lived, but was confused as to why the buildings were in ruins and why there was no garden. During her teenage years, Eady spent every available moment studying Egyptology, which included learning to interpret hieroglyphics with the legendary Sir Ernest Wallis Budge, Keeper of Egyptian Antiquities at the British Museum. But Eady would have to wait until she was twenty-nine-years old, and the wife of an Egyptian student, before she could see Egypt. There she became the first woman ever to work for the Egyptian Antiquities Department, and had a son from her marriage, whom she named Sety. In keeping with the Egyptian custom of not referring to women by their first name, Eady was then known as Omm Sety, "mother of Sety." Many years afterward, in 1956, her marriage over, she finally traveled "home" to Abydos, where she was to remain, living in a small peasant house until her death in 1981.

Built by Sety I (the pharaoh Sethos I, reigned 1318–1304 BCE), the temple at Abydos became a place of religious devotion for Eady. She would remove her shoes before entering the building and once inside, worship the ancient Egyptian gods in the ancient manner. It was mainly through her dreams, which she recorded in

DOROTHY LOUISE EADY

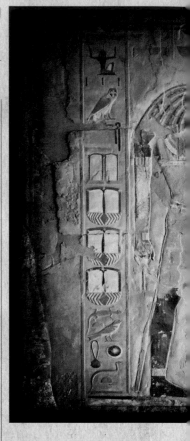

detail in her diaries using a form of automatic writing, that she came to believe that she was the reincarnation of a fourteen-year-old virgin priestess called Bentreshyt, who had lived at the Temple of Abydos during the reign of Sety I.

Eady believed her main role as Bentreshyt was to play a part in the dramatized rituals of the death and resurrection of the Egyptian god Osiris, which were held at the Temple. She claimed that Sety I had fallen in love with her after the two met by chance in the Temple gardens when she had been a young priestess there. Bentreshyt's story has a predictably tragic end as she discovered she was pregnant after the liaison, and, rather than expose the Pharaoh to ridicule, she committed suicide.

Due to her knowledge of all things Egyptian, Eady became a popular and respected figure at Abydos: socializing, giving tours of the ruins, writing papers, and apparently passing on the secrets of ancient Egyptian magic and healing to locals who came to see her. The most fascinating part of the story, however, is the archaeological discoveries at Abydos which were allegedly made based on channeled "memories" of Bentreshyt's time at the temple more than three thousand years before.

Eady's most widely publicized claim was that there had once been

a garden attached to the ancient Temple of Sety I. Though the majority of ancient Egyptian temples possessed gardens, Eady was apparently able to pinpoint the exact spot in which to dig for the ruins, and also predicted the discovery of a tunnel running underneath the northern part of the Temple, which was indeed proven to be the case by subsequent archaeological excavation on the site. Another more controversial

Left **Fresco at Hatshepsut Temple in Egypt.**

SEE ALSO

Channeling **Pages 77–81**
Automatic writing
Pages 97–102

prediction—that underneath the Temple of Sety I there lies a secret vault containing a library of hidden historical and religious records—has yet to be tested by excavation. Eady was an unusual and colorful woman, whose detailed knowledge of Egyptology and ancient Egyptian magical and religious practices was respected by all who met her, including the numerous Egyptologists who worked alongside her at Abydos.

Many researchers are of the opinion that it would have been difficult, though not impossible, for her to obtain such a profound knowledge and understanding of ancient Egypt through normal channels of learning. Though her bizarre claim can never be proven, there is no question that Eady believed she was channeling the spirit of Bentreshyt, the Temple virgin who had lived at Abydos during the fourteenth century BCE.

AURIC SIGHT

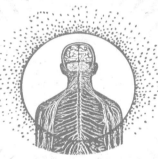

The aura is believed by New Agers, psychics, and mystics to be a type of organic energy field which surrounds the bodies of all living things. Certain people who are able to see the aura using their "third eye" describe a luminous colored outline emanating from the surface of a person or an object. Indeed, auras have been compared to the aureoles or halos of saints and angels used in Christian art to depict the radiance associated with divine or spiritual light.

The belief in the existence of a human aura is an ancient one. During the Medieval period, four distinct types of aura were identified: the nimbus, the halo, the aureola, and the glory. The first two of these emanate from the head, while the aureola streams from the whole body; the glory is a combination of the two.

Some psychics, such as Matthew Manning (see page 22) and Edgar Cayce (see Medical Intuition, pages 114–119), have claimed to be able to interpret the physical and/or mental health of a person by "reading" their aura. A bright or clear aura indicates better mental and emotional health than a dull or muddy one, for example. Specific colors seen in a person's aura by those skilled in aura-reading are also interpreted as a guide to their emotions and physiology. Though there

Halos have been used in the iconography of many religions to indicate holy or sacred figures.

are no hard and fast rules among psychics as to which colors of the aura represent a particular emotional state, there is a general guide. Apparently, the majority of people have one or two colors which dominate their aura. Brilliant red is said to indicate the physical body, anger and force, a darker red passion and sensuality; brown represents greed; yellow well-being and a high level of intellectual activity; purple spirituality and intuition; blue religious devotion and spirituality; green dishonesty and jealousy; and dark green sympathy. Some psychics note that just before a person dies their aura becomes the color white and increases in intensity.

GENERAL GUIDE TO AURAS

Brilliant red: physical body, anger, and force

Dark red: passion and sensuality

Brown: greed

Yellow: well-being and high intellectual activity

Purple: spirituality and intuition

Green: dishonesty and jealousy

Dark green: sympathy

Intense white: before a person dies

Blue: religious devotion and spirituality

In the 1840s, chemist Baron Carl von Reichenbach (1788–1869) carried out experiments with mediums who claimed to be able to see a glow over the bodies of the sick in hospitals, and a fainter column of light over newly made graves. Von Reichenbach also experimented with magnets and crystals and found the same mysterious aura associated with them. He christened the mysterious emanations "the odic force."

The most important early experiments into the aura were carried out by Dr. Walter John Kilner (1847–1920), a medical electrician at St. Thomas' Hospital, London. In 1911 Kilner published a book on his work on the human aura, *The Human Atmosphere, or the Aura Made Visible by the Aid of Chemical Screens*. In this work Kilner proposed the existence of the aura and its possible use in medical diagnosis, arguing that the human aura, or energy field, is a guide to health and mood. He also attempted to invent equipment which could train the naked eye to observe activity in the human aura.

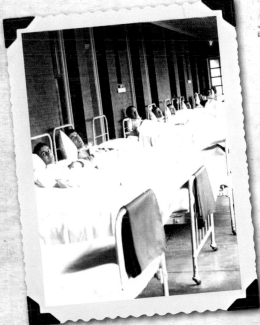

Skeptics have criticized clairvoyants and psychics who claim to be able to see and photograph the human aura for offering no scientific evidence to support their claims. Critics argue that while it is known that the human body does indeed emit radiations, for example weak electromagnetic discharges from the electrical activity of the nerves, and sonic waves from the physical actions inside the body, these activities do not represent one unified phenomenon, as psychics insist the aura is. Another objection to this argument is that no two psychics will describe seeing the same aura: some will see multiple layers of an entire aura, while others will see only one layer or only parts of an aura.

The odic force idea was never favored among mainstream scientists.

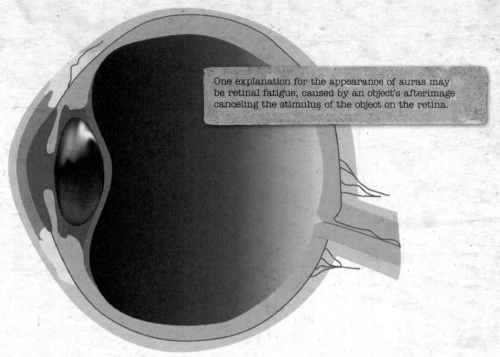

One explanation for the appearance of auras may be retinal fatigue, caused by an object's afterimage canceling the stimulus of the object on the retina.

In an attempt to test the claims of an aura-reader, James Randi set up an experiment which was shown as part of a TV special aired in 1989, called *Exploring Psychic Powers Live!* A US$100,000 prize was offered for a successful demonstration of the reality of aura reading. The psychic who was being tested selected ten people whose auras were clearly visible to her. There were ten numbered screens on the stage, short enough for the aura of the person who was to stand behind it to be seen by the psychic. An unspecified number of the volunteers were asked to stand behind the screens, and the psychic was asked to use her aura reading power to identify which screens concealed a person. The psychic stated that she saw auras over all ten screens; unfortunately for her, only four of the screens had someone standing behind them. In other words her "powers" produced results no better than chance.

A number of non-mystical explanations for the appearance of the aura around an object or person have been put forward by scientists. The most straightforward of these is that if a person stares at an object against a white background in low light for long enough, the "aura" that they see is actually the result of retinal fatigue, rather than any special psychic powers. A condition known as synaesthesia, which is probably caused by a "cross-wiring" in the brain, may also explain why some people see auras. With synaesthesia, the stimulation of one sense produces a response in other senses, so for example when a person with synaesthesia hears a sound they may also experience smells at the same time. A number of synaesthetes also see colors when looking at numbers or letters. One in 200 people suffer from synaesthesia, so perhaps a percentage of those people claiming to be able to see auras are in fact suffering from synesthesia.

HOW TO

TEST FOR AURIC SIGHT

1. HOW MANY PEOPLE ARE KNOWN TO HAVE HAD THIS POWER?

It is not a commonly recorded power—so relatively few.

2. HOW IS THE POWER ACQUIRED?

Some psychics claim that a person can learn to develop auric vision.

3. WHAT ARE THE EARLY WARNING SIGNS?

Being able to perceive a faint glow surrounding people, animals, and objects.

4. HOW DO I KNOW IF I HAVE THE POTENTIAL TO DEVELOP THIS POWER?

If you have an intense awareness of other people's feelings, and perhaps a strong reaction to certain colors.

5. WHAT MATERIALS WILL I NEED FOR THE TEST?

None.

6. WHAT ARE THE DANGERS ASSOCIATED WITH THIS POWER?

There are none. It's good to be in tune with other people's auras.

TEST

SEE ANOTHER PERSON'S AURA

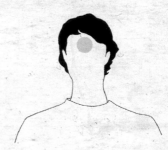

According to many psychics, being able to see another person's aura is not particularly difficult, in fact with a little practice and concentration, we can all see them.

[1] Choose a quiet time of the day in comfortable surroundings where there are few distractions.

[2] Find a willing and open-minded person to work with.

[4] Focus on the middle of the subject's forehead (their "third eye" according to mystics), and concentrate on this spot for 30–60 seconds. Resist the temptation to look elsewhere.

[5] Soon you will notice that the background directly behind the subject is far brighter and perhaps even has a different color than the background farther away. This is the person's "aura."

[6] With more focus the aura will become clearer and you will begin to discern more colors.

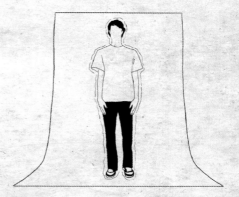

[3] Position the subject in front of a plain white background.

KIRLIAN PHOTOGRAPHY

While working in a hospital in Krasnodor, Russia, in 1939, electrician Semyon Kirlian accidentally discovered that if an object is placed on a photographic plate and subjected to a high-voltage electric field, an image surrounded by a colored halo is created on the plate. "The Kirlian effect" as it became known, was heralded by parapsychologists as finally providing proof of the reality of the aura. Along with his wife Valentina, Kirlian developed the technique and soon there were several different methods for obtaining Kirlian photographs of the human aura. One method involves the object, animate or inanimate, being placed on the emulsion side of a color film which is then positioned between a high voltage plate electrode and an earthed plate electrode, causing an electrical discharge to take place. No camera is used. Kirlian photographs of animate objects show auras that constantly change color and vary in size and shape, while inanimate objects display more consistent halos.

A Kirlian photo being taken of a leaf.

KIRLIAN PHOTOGRAPHY

One particularly well-known Kirlian photograph shows an ivy leaf which, despite having had its tip severed prior to being photographed, shows the missing piece still present as an after image or "apparition." This "phantom leaf" photograph and others like it have persuaded some parapsychologists that the aura is a manifestation of a mysterious organizing energy permeating all life-forms. Some researchers have even suggested a connection between death and the afterlife,

The aura of the cut-off section of this leaf appears to be "restored" by Kirlian photography.

and reports of ghosts of the recently deceased.

However, critics of Kirlian photography are quick to point out that if the whole leaf is pressed firmly onto the film before any part of it is removed, the "apparition" merely represents residue from the amputated section. As living things are moist, this moisture will be transferred to the emulsion surface of the photographic film, causing a change in the electric charge pattern on the film. For such "phantom leaf" photographs to be taken seriously, the leaf would have to be cut before there is any contact with the film. Skeptics also insist that rather than showing the "life-energy" of a person or an object, Kirlian photographs are merely an image of a corona discharge in a gas, most commonly the ambient air.

According to the (admittedly unreliable) book about ESP research in Russia, *Psychic Discoveries—The Iron Curtain Lifted* (1997) by Sheila Ostrander and Lynn Schroeder, by the 1980s in Russia, Kirlian photography was second only to X-ray in use as a diagnostic tool. Apparently doctors would regularly examine the changing colors of a patient's auras to gain unique insights into their physical and mental illnesses.

Current research into aura photography in Russia is being carried out by Dr. Konstantin Korotkov, Deputy Director of Saint-Petersburg Scientific-Research Institute of Physical Culture, and Professor of Computer Systems Design at the St. Petersburg State Technical

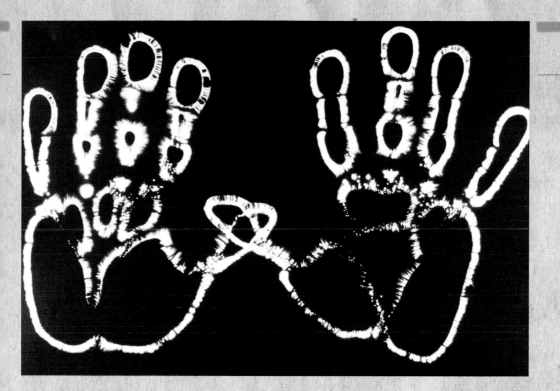

**Kirlian photo.
Bio-electric discharges
revealing illnesses, or
psychosomatic states.**

University of Information
Technologies, Mechanics and
Optics. Korotkov's research uses
Gas Discharge Visualization
(GDV), which is based on the
Kirlian effect. He has published
a number of books on the subject,
including *Light After Life:
Experiments and Ideas on
After-Death Changes of Kirlian
Pictures* (1998).

In the 1970s and 1980s in
the US, parapsychologist Dr
Thelma Moss of the UCLA
Neuropsychiatric Institute
proposed Kirlian photography as
a tool in medical diagnosis and
brought the subject to public
attention with the publication of
her books *The Body Electric* (1979),
and *The Probability of the Impossible*
(1983). Moss carried out a number
of experiments to investigate various
aspects of the human aura, one of
which examined how a person's
strong emotions, such as love and
anger, were reflected in the subtle
changes in the color of their aura.

SEE ALSO

Extrasensory perception
Pages 17–21
Auric sight **Pages 87–92**

AUTOMATIC WRITING

utomatic writing is the process of producing scripts that do not originate in the conscious thoughts of the writer. Many of its proponents claim that the material produced may come from discarnate entities, sometimes referred to as "spirit guides." The first recorded case of what may be called automatic writing comes from the Bible (1 Chronicles 28: 1–19). This text relates the story of the building of the first temple (the "Temple of Solomon") on Mount Moriah, Jerusalem. David gives his son, Solomon, the plan of the vestibule of the temple, its houses, treasuries, upper rooms, inner chambers, and of the room for the mercy seat. David then states that "All this he made clear to me in writing from the hand of the Lord, all the work to be done according to the plan."

The popularity of automatic writing soared with the appearance of the spiritualist movement in the late nineteenth century, when it became a popular technique of divination. It was during this period that British medium and Church of England minister William Stainton Moses (1839–92), produced a staggering 24 volumes of automatic writing (extracted from his notebooks), which were edited by Frederic W.H. Myers in a book called *Spirit Teachings* (1883).

King Solomon oversees the building of the first temple on Mount Mariah.

great loss of life. Twenty years later, in April 1912, the RMS *Titanic* hit an iceberg and went down in the North Atlantic. Stead was on board and died in the disaster.

Perhaps the strangest of all automatic writing practitioners was late-nineteenth-century medium Hélène Smith (real name Catherine Müller). Smith also claimed she had been an Indian Princess and Marie Antoinette in past lives on earth. In the early years of the twentieth century, Swiss Psychology Professor, Théodore Flournoy investigated Smith's claim that she had visited Mars and that her automatic writing carried messages from the inhabitants of the planet in the Martian language. Flournoy soon realized, however, that her "Martian" language was remarkably similar to her native French. Nevertheless, Flournoy's book on Smith's fantastical claims, *From India to the Planet Mars* (1901), still makes interesting and entertaining reading.

Above: W.T. Stead photographed with his family in 1891.
Right: Martian language.

English campaigning journalist William Thomas Stead, editor of the *Pall Mall Gazette* between 1883 and 1889, claimed that he received messages via a spirit contact named Julia. He also produced automatic writing, though in a somewhat unusual way. Stead used automatic writing to communicate with living people who were a great distance away, posing a question to a certain person in his mind and receiving the reply in the form of automatic writing. During the process he claimed that his hand was being guided by the other person in spite of the great distance separating them. In 1892, Stead published an article in the *London Review of Reviews* entitled "From the Old World to the New," which told of a great liner colliding with an iceberg in the North Atlantic and sinking with

Through automatic writing, Manning obtained tips from his great-grandfather for the Grand National.

Perhaps the most prolific of all practitioners of automatic writing was Chico Xavier (1910–2002), a well-known medium in Brazil's spiritulism movement. Xavier wrote around 400 books using automatic writing, claiming that a wide variety of discarnate authors were responsible for the work and that he was merely the conduit through which these authors worked.

Matthew Manning was famous for his use of automatic writing in the early 1970s to record messages from long-dead inhabitants of his house (see page 22). Manning also claimed that on one occasion, in order to try and find some names of winning horses at Ascot,

he "contacted" his great-grandfather—Hayward Collins—a racehorse owner. On the day of the races, the family deliberately avoided looking at the papers to check which horses were running. Through automatic writing Hayward gave six names, all of which proved to be running. Of the six given, five finished within the first three and two won. Some time later, Matthew received some race tips for the British Grand National from Collins—he predicted Red Rum to win, Crisp to come second, and advised leaving third place well alone as it was too close. This turned out to be the exact result—third place was a photo-finish.

FAMOUS CASES OF AUTOMATIC WRITERS

- ✪ DAVID AND SOLOMON (c. TENTH CENTURY BCE)
- ✪ MADAME HELENA PETROVNA BLAVATSKY (1813–1891)
- ✪ ALFRED RUSSELL WALLACE (1823–1913)
- ✪ THE REV. WILLIAM STAINTON MOSES (1839–92)
- ✪ W.T. STEAD (1849–1912)
- ✪ HÉLÈNE SMITH (1861–1929)
- ✪ ALICE BAILEY (1880–1949)
- ✪ PEARL CURRAN ("PATIENCE WORTH") (1883–1937)
- ✪ CHICO XAVIER (1910–2002)
- ✪ MATTHEW MANNING (1955–)

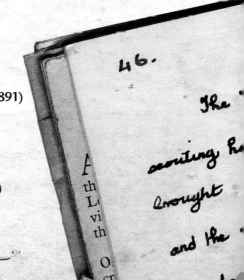

Above: Elizabeth Hope, known as Elizabeth d'Esperance, with a "materialized spirit."

Some occult writers, Madame Blavatsky (1813–1891), and Alice Bailey (1880–1949), for example, have attributed the origin of their automatic writing scripts to discarnate "Tibetan Masters" or "Inner Plane entities," though more skeptical writers on the subject would point to a much more prosaic source for the material. Indeed, it is not exactly clear whether automatic writing can be classified as a supernatural ability at all. Isn't it more likely that the writer is tapping into a different level of their own consciousness? Whether there is a paranormal factor involved in the process of automatic writing will always be almost impossible to determine. This is because researchers cannot know for certain whether the information being "received" has not been locked away in some hidden recess of the practitioner's subconscious all the time, only to emerge when the person is in a certain mental state. This explanation appears to be more believable than messages being "dictated" by discarnate spirits.

Although most mediums who practice automatic writing are often in a trance state when they record their messages from the beyond, others like Pearl Lenore Curran (see page 103), were aware of their surroundings though not always of the actions of their writing hand. Sometimes, as was the case with the medium Madame Elizabeth D'Esperance (1855–1919), the writer feels a prickling or tingling sensation in their arm as the "messages" are about to come through. William Stainton Moses described his right arm being seized and "dashed violently up and down." He was, he said "powerless to interfere." Nineteenth-century British author and pioneer spiritualist, William Howitt, described something akin to an electric shock running through his arm and hand and the pencil moving in circles apparently of its own volition.

HOW TO

TEST FOR AUTOMATIC WRITING

1. HOW MANY PEOPLE ARE KNOWN TO HAVE HAD THIS POWER?

Although a number of nineteenth-century mediums claimed this power, it is relatively rare these days.

2. HOW IS THE POWER ACQUIRED?

Some people with this ability have always had it, though others have acquired it suddenly, without explanation.

3. WHAT ARE THE EARLY WARNING SIGNS?

Tingling sensation in your arms, perhaps a feeling akin to a mild electric shock running through the body.

4. HOW DO I KNOW IF I HAVE THE POTENTIAL TO DEVELOP THIS POWER?

You are able to unconsciously write down numerous pages of text without explanation.

5. WHAT MATERIALS WILL I NEED FOR THE TEST?

Pen, and paper, or computer.

6. WHAT ARE THE DANGERS ASSOCIATED WITH THIS POWER?

You might find out things from deceased loved ones which may be upsetting.

TEST

AUTOMATIC WRITING

[1] Decide on the purpose of your automatic writing exercise—do you want to try and make contact with a discarnate entity? Do you want merely to see what will happen when your unconscious takes over?

[2] Take a supply of paper and a pen and sit in a comfortable position at a desk. The pen should be gently held above the paper.

[3] Relax, and try to clear your mind of all thought other than the writing you want to carry out.

[4] According to psychics, if you are attempting to contact a specific entity it is at this stage that the help of this entity should be requested. Keep all requests simple—start by calling their name, for example.

[5] When messages begin to come through, write everything down, even if it appears not to make sense. Over time you will learn how to interpret messages and the meaning of your text will become clearer.

PEARL LENORE CURRAN

Patience Worth was the pen name used by St. Louis housewife Pearl Lenore Curran to compose a bewildering variety of novels, poems, and prose during the early part of the twentieth century. What is almost unique about Patience Worth is that Curren claimed that she was the spirit of a seventeenth-century English girl who channeled her thoughts and ideas through her.

Curran was born Pearl Lenore Pollard in Mound City, Illinois, on February 15, 1883. The family later moved to Texas and then to St. Louis when Curran was 14. Academically below average, the young girl did possess a talent for music, taking lessons and training in piano and voice. When Curran was 24, she married John Howard Curran, living a comfortable and uneventful middle-class existence in St. Louis.

In August 1912, one of Curran's neighbors showed her a Ouija board, and despite Curran's reservations, persuaded her to place her hands on it. Although the results were negative the ladies continued their experiments, occasionally receiving vague "communications" through the board, but nothing meaningful. Then on July 8, 1913, a message began to come through, it read: "Many moons ago I lived. Again I come. Patience Worth is my name. If thou shalt live, so shall I." This message was to be the beginning of a 25-year period during which the "entity" known as Patience Worth communicated to the world, apparently through Curran. As Pearl became more and more interested in the numerous messages from Patience, she began spending more time on the Ouija board. However, it soon became apparent that the Ouija board method was far too slow and cumbersome to deal with the vast amount of material being received, so Curran turned to direct automatic writing.

Pearl Lenore Curran clamied she was the spirit of a seventeeth-century English girl.

PEARL LENORE CURRAN

In common with William Stainton Moses, Curran never went into a trance to record the messages. The method she used was to sit in a brightly lit room and wait for the sentences to form in her mind while in a conscious state, and then write or type them out. While the words poured into her head, Curran would feel pressure and soon scenes and images would present themselves before her. She was then able to note the details of each scene, the road, trees, landscape, and people. Occasionally she would see herself in the scenes.

One difficulty Curran experienced was that the messages were received in a dialect which was often difficult to understand. This was partly explained when she learned from her communications that Patience Worth was a young girl who had lived on a farm in the county of Dorset, on the south coast of England, in the 1600s. Patience's family had subsequently emigrated to America and she had been murdered by Indians there. In all the years of communicating with Patience Worth, this is all that Curran ever found out about her.

In 1916, Casper Yost's book, *Patience Worth: A Psychic Mystery*, was published. Yost was editor of the *St. Louis Globe-Democrat*, and had promoted Curran's claims of contact with Patience Worth in a series of articles in the paper beginning in February 1915. William Marion Reedy, the editor of the weekly St. Louis-based journal *Reedy's Mirror*, also became a convert and published glowing articles about Patience Worth's literary creations. The result of this publicity was that the name of Patience Worth soon became known throughout the world.

In the 25 years for which she was "communicating," Patience Worth dictated a vast amount of literary work to Curran, including six novels, hundreds of pages of poetry, proverbs, prayers, and conversation. Many of her works were published under the name Patience Worth, including the novels *The Sorry Tale, A Story of the Time of Christ, Telka, An Idyl of Medieval England*, and *Hope Trueblood: A Nineteenth-Century Tale*. Many critics, including those from *The New York Times* and *The Bookman*, were impressed not only by the beauty of some of the imagery, but also by her use of archaic languages and words. How, they wondered, could a modest St. Louis housewife have

Above **Pearl and Patience together wrote several novels, short stories and many poems.**

acquired such precise historical details and such sophisticated literary skill?

Others were perhaps more perceptive, noting that the appearance of Patience Worth coincided with a revival of spiritualism in Europe and America, creating an environment where many members of the public were only too willing to believe in the reality of the reincarnation of a seventeenth-century British girl in twentieth-

century St. Louis. The skeptics also wondered how Patience, supposedly a resident of seventeenth-century England, managed to dictate a novel set in the Victorian era (*Hope Trueblood*).

After 1922, communications from Patience began to decrease and eventually stopped altogether. Interest in the phenomenon of Patience Worth soon faded as well, and when Curran died in 1939, both she and her communicator were virtually unknown. Perhaps because there was never a solution to the mystery and no proof was

Above **Pearl Curran visualized the English countryside where Patience grew up in the 1600s.**

ever produced that a girl named Patience Worth actually existed in seventeenth-century Dorset, the case is regarded with skepticism by most psychical researchers today.

But the question remains—was there a spirit from the beyond speaking through Pearl Curran? Or, as seems more likely, was it all a product of Pearl's unconscious

mind? The case was meticulously investigated at the time by Dr. Walter Franklin Prince, research officer of the American Society for Psychical Research from 1920–1924, and in his summing up of the case he allowed that "some cause operating through but not originating in the subconscious of Mrs. Curran" could be responsible for the phenomenon of Patience Worth. Perhaps the progress currently being made by scientists and psychologists in studies of the human personality and its various idiosyncrasies will one day shed more light on the strange appearance of Patience Worth.

SEE ALSO

Retrocognition **Pages 59–63**
Automatic writing
Pages 97–102

PSYCHOMETRY

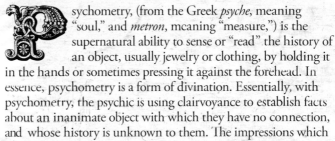

Psychometry, (from the Greek *psyche*, meaning "soul," and *metron*, meaning "measure,") is the supernatural ability to sense or "read" the history of an object, usually jewelry or clothing, by holding it in the hands or sometimes pressing it against the forehead. In essence, psychometry is a form of divination. Essentially, with psychometry, the psychic is using clairvoyance to establish facts about an inanimate object with which they have no connection, and whose history is unknown to them. The impressions which the "sensitive" receives from the object are usually perceived as images, though sounds, smells, tastes, and occasionally emotions are sometimes sensed.

But how does psychometry work? Some parapsychologists hypothesize that any object has an associated energy field that transfers details of its history which certain people who are "tuned in" can read. New Age author, Rosemary Ellen Guiley, believes that all objects are filled with the vibrations transferred to them from past human actions and emotions. If this is the case then the object in effect functions like a tape recorder, storing information which can be played back at a later date. Other researchers are of the opinion that it is not the object that the psychic is reading but the

Opposite: US psychic Peter Nelson performing psychometry experiment, 1984.
Left: Rosemary Ellen Guiley, New Age author.

the discovery of psychometry, he has found a new science, that of "soul measuring."

From his research, Buchanan concluded that all objects have "souls" that retain a memory imprinted on them by human emotions. He believed that the entire history of the world was contained in these inanimate objects, just waiting to be decoded by the psychic. As he put it:

person, the object functioning merely as a focusing device to prevent loss of concentration.

The term "psychometry" was coined in 1842 by Joseph Rodes Buchanan, a professor of physiology at the Eclectic Medical Institute in Covington, Kentucky. In his *Manual of Psychometry: The Dawn of a New Civilization* (1885), Buchanan states his belief that in

> . . . it literally signifies soul-measuring, being analogous to the words, thermometry, barometry, electrometry, and similar terms, which signify special measurements. The thermometer measures caloric (thermo, temperature). The barometer measures the weight (baro, weight) of the atmosphere; the electrometer measures electric conditions; the psychometer measures the soul (psyche).

Manual of Psychometry: The Dawn of a New Civilization, 1893

> The Past is entombed in the Present! The world is its own enduring monument; and that which is true of its physical, is likewise true of its mental career. The discoveries of Psychometry will enable us to explore the history of man, as those of geology enable us to explore the history of the earth. There are mental fossils for psychologists as well as mineral fossils for the geologists; and I believe that hereafter the psychologist and the geologist will go hand in hand—the one portraying the earth, its animals and its vegetation, while the other portrays the human beings who have roamed over its surface in the shadows, and the darkness of primeval barbarism! Aye, the mental telescope is now discovered which may pierce the depths of the past and bring us in full view of the grand and tragic passages of ancient history!

Manual of Psychometry: The Dawn of a New Civilization, 1893

In more recent times, psychometry has allegedly been used by law enforcement agencies in the form of "psychic detectives" (see page 112). The majority of the evidence for the effectiveness of these psychic detectives is, however, provided either by the psychic themselves, or the mass media, rather than by an objective independent source. Indeed, a number of police departments around the world have issued official statements to the effect that they do not regard the work of psychics as trustworthy or effective on cases. In 1978, Martin Reisert, director of the behavioral science section of the Los Angeles Police Department, tested 12 psychics by questioning them regarding evidence shown to them in connection with four crimes. The report of the controlled test showed practically no evidence of the reality of psychometry or any other psychic ability.

Above: Walter F. Prince, American psychical researcher, President of the SPR 1930–1931.

From 1919–1922 German physician and psychical researcher Gustav Pagenstecher (1855–1942) carried out research into psychometry in Mexico City, after he had discovered that a patient, Maria Reyes Zierold, could apparently see beyond the closed doors of her room and describe what was happening outside. Maria also claimed that when she held objects they gave her sensations of vision, smell, taste, hearing, or emotions. A medical committee in Mexico City found Zierold's abilities unexplainable, and while visiting Mexico in 1921, Walter Franklin Prince, principal research officer of the American Society for Psychical Research (SPR), came to similar conclusions.

HOW TO

TEST FOR PSYCHOMETRY

1. HOW MANY PEOPLE ARE KNOWN TO HAVE HAD THIS POWER?

It is not particularly common, though there have been a number of "psychic detectives" over the last few decades who have allegedly utilized this power.

2. HOW IS THE POWER ACQUIRED?

This is unusally a congenital ability, though some claim to have acquired it suddenly without warning.

3. WHAT ARE THE EARLY WARNING SIGNS?

Unexplained sensations (flashes of imagery) when touching certain objects.

4. HOW DO I KNOW IF I HAVE THE POTENTIAL TO DEVELOP THIS POWER?

If you are able to "see" events, or people related to an object merely from touching it.

5. WHAT MATERIALS WILL I NEED FOR THE TEST?

An extra person and one or two personal objects associated with them.

6. WHAT ARE THE DANGERS ASSOCIATED WITH THIS POWER?

There are none. This can be a very interesting power to possess.

PSYCHOMETRY

TEST

THE ARTIFACT TEST

This test requires a quiet location where you will not be disturbed, and one other person.

[1] Sit in a comfortable position, with your eyes closed. Try to relax.

[2] Without saying anything, the other person places an object in your hands. Do not open your eyes.

[3] Take the object, the history of which is unknown to you, but known to the other person. Ideally the object should be something personal, belonging to that person, that they have owned for a long time. Alternatively, an archaeological artifact whose date and background is known, for example a piece of Roman pottery or jewelry.

6] When you are ready, describe what you see or feel, images, impressions, smells, tastes, out loud to the other person. Don't worry how strange or irrelevant your impressions may be, they may be important to the owner of the object.

[7] When you are ready, open your eyes and return the object to its owner. Discuss with them to determine how accurate your impressions were. Don't be discouraged if you are inaccurate the first few times, Parapsychologists say that the talent of psychometry can be improved with practice.

[4] Hold the object in your hand or press it to your forehead.

[5] Relax, do not force yourself to think, let images come into your mind as they will.

GERARD CROISET

Also known as Gerard Boekbinder, Dutch psychic Gerard Croiset (1909–1980) was a controversial figure who gained a reputation as a psychic detective from the 1940s until his death in 1980. While a young man working for a watch repairer, Croiset held a ruler which belonged to his employer, and immediately began to "see" events from the man's life, which were later confirmed to be accurate. Croiset allegedly used his powers of psychometry to help police departments not only in his native Netherlands but also in the US, Australia, and Puerto Rico, solving a number of puzzling crimes and locating hundreds of missing persons. In one unspecified Dutch case, Croiset is said to have studied the personal possessions of a murdered woman, and provided police with accurate information regarding her murder, including the name of her murderer, a man already being held in connection with the crime.

On one occasion Croiset's help was enlisted in the search for a missing four-year-old girl from Brooklyn, New York. Croiset was sent a photo of the girl, an item of her clothing, and a map of New York City. Using psychometry he concluded that she was dead, identified the location of her body and the name of the man who murdered her. Croiset's information apparently led to the recovery of the girl's body and to the conviction of the murderer for the crime.

In another successful case in May 1976, Croiset was flown from Holland to Japan by a Japanese television station to see if he could help locate a missing seven-year-old girl. After being shown a picture of the missing girl, Miwa Kikuchi, Croiset stated that she was dead and "on the surface of a lake near her home and near a quay for boats near a yellow protruding structure." The girl's body was later recovered floating in the reservoir near a quay for rowing boats and a water supply tower, which was painted yellow. Although the press were astounded at Croiset's paranormal abilities, some police officers stated that they would have found the girl's body without the help of Croiset's clairvoyance.

The details of Croiset's extraordinary career were recorded by Dutch parapsychologist Wilhelm Tenhaeff (1894–1981), director of the Parapsychology Institute of the State University of Utrecht.

Left **Eric Cutler at the home of Gerard Croiset in 1970, seeking advice on a missing woman.**

Tenhaeff "discovered" Croiset in 1945 when he was running a small healing clinic, and, amazed by the psychic's abilities, he spent much of his time testing and developing them. It was Tenhaeff who started Croiset on his path to psychic superstardom by contacting the

Dutch police and offering them Croiset's help with puzzling unsolved cases. However, it later emerged that Tenhaeff had been doctoring the data on his research and testing of Croiset, and also exaggerating his successes as a psychic sleuth while ignoring his many failures.

For example, in 1966 Croiset was invited to Australia to help locate the three missing Beaumont children who had disappeared from a beach in Adelaide, South Australia. Although Croiset attracted much media attention while in the country, and had his expenses paid by a wealthy businessman, his conviction that the children would be found within half a mile of where they had last been seen proved to be incorrect and they were never discovered.

The following year Croiset was called in by the police in Scotland, regarding the disappearance of Patricia McAdam in 1967 while she was hitching a lift with a friend in a lorry from Glasgow to Dumfries. Croiset told police that the girl's body had been thrown in a river, but after a thorough search nothing was discovered, and in fact McAdam's body was never found.

SEE ALSO

Clairvoyance **Pages 37–44**
Psychometry **Pages 107–111**

MEDICAL INTUITION

Medical intuition is a form of clairvoyance where the medical intuitive uses their "sixth sense" to perceive a physical or emotional ailment inside the body of a patient. After the medical intuitive has diagnosed the patient's illness using their intuition, they will either treat the problem themselves or pass the information on to the patient's medical doctor for further evaluation. Although some medical intuitives are also M.D.s, the majority are not licensed medical professionals. The term "medical intuitive" was first introduced by Dr. Norm Shealy and Dr. Caroline Myss in 1987, as part of Shealy's research into intuition and medical application. Myss is herself a medical intuitive, and has authored a number of books on the subject, including *The Creation of Health* (1988), *Anatomy of the Spirit* (1996), and *Why People Don't Heal and How They Can* (1998).

The magnificently named Phineas Parkhurst Quimby (1802–1866), is generally recognized as the first documented case of an intuitive healer. However, it is Edgar Cayce (1877–1945), a Kentucky-born psychic and healer known as the "Sleeping Prophet," who

Nineteenth-century wood engraving of Phineas P. Quimby, American medical-intuitive healer.

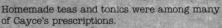
Homemade teas and tonics were among many of Cayce's prescriptions.

remains to this day the best known of all medical intuitives, or a "medical clairvoyant" as he was known. Cayce's diagnoses would involve him going into a self-induced hypnotic trance, after which the patient's condition would be "described" to him. A diagnosis expressed in medical terminology would follow and then a recommendation for treatment.

From the very beginning, Cayce and his associates insisted that the treatments be administered by local doctors with access to the patients. Many of Cayce's prescriptions were extremely simple: massage, relaxation, tonics, diet, poultices, exercises, plasters, and homemade teas and tonics. Cayce's philosophy behind his trance healing work was a holistic one, meaning that he saw the body as a "system," an interconnected network of organs and tissue, and if one

part was not functioning properly then it would affect the rest. In essence, Cayce would treat the cause and not the effect, helping the health of the entire system in order to defeat the disorder, although suggestion would surely have played a major part in his successful treatment of patients.

The main difficulty that the scientific and medical community have with medical intuitives is the complete lack of peer-reviewed scientific studies which support their claims. Medical intuitives argue that because their skill is not a science, it therefore cannot be tested scientifically. However, it is fairly easy to set up an experiment to prove whether or not the diagnoses of medical intuitives are accurate significantly beyond the rate of chance. It is indeed curious that so few medical intuitives have made the

THE WORK OF EDGAR CAYCE:
THE SLEEPING PROPHET

At Edgar Cayce's death in 1945 there were over 14,000 stenographic records of his trance readings for over 8,000 patients. The Association for Research and Enlightenment, founded in 1931 in Virginia Beach, Virginia, is now the international headquarters for the work of Edgar Cayce, and holds copies of over 14,000 of Edgar Cayce's readings all of which are available to the public.

effort to do this and prove that their ability is genuine. So, while there may be something significant in the claims of a few medical intuitives, until more practitioners submit their abilities to controlled experiments medical intuition will continue to be dismissed by medical professionals as a combination of suggestion by the practitioner, and wishful thinking on the part of the patient.

HOW TO

TEST MEDICAL INTUITION

1. HOW MANY PEOPLE ARE KNOWN TO HAVE HAD THIS POWER?

Not many, it is a very rare power.

2. HOW IS THE POWER ACQUIRED?

Although people are usually born with this ability are born with it, a few (Edgar Cayce for example) have acquired it suddenly after surgery or trauma.

3. WHAT ARE THE EARLY WARNING SIGNS?

The sensation that you can "see" inside a person and identify what is wrong with them.

4. HOW DO I KNOW IF I HAVE THE POTENTIAL TO DEVELOP THIS POWER?

If you are repeatedly able to identify people's ailments without prior knowledge of their condition.

5. WHAT MATERIALS WILL I NEED FOR THE TEST?

None.

6. WHAT ARE THE DANGERS ASSOCIATED WITH THIS POWER?

There are many dangers associated with the alleged possession of this power, but the main one is giving people who are suffering from serious diseases misleading medical information or false hope.

TEST

DEVELOP MEDICAL INTUITION

Medical intuitives often assess the physical health, energy fields, and emotional states of their clients using muscle testing (kinesiology).

You can try this simple test yourself.

[1] You will need at least 4 people to do this test.

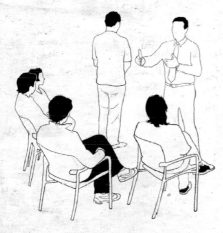

[2] Ask one of the people (the subject) to stand up while the remaining people (the audience) sit down.

[3] This person should then stand with their back to the audience and extend their arm perpendicular to their body. In this test the person's arm is known as the "indicator muscle."

[4] Without letting the subject see your hand, give either a thumbs up sign or a thumbs down sign to the audience. Thumbs up indicates that everyone should smile and think positive thoughts. Thumbs down means they should think bad or negative thoughts about the subject.

[5] Using the arm as a testing muscle, see if the subject can hold their arm up as you lightly pull down on their wrist during the thumbs-up test and the thumbs-down test.

[6] According to medical intuitives the negative feelings of the audience should make the indicator muscle weak and it will thus be impossible for the test subject to hold their arm in position for very long during the thumbs down part of the experiment. The positive thoughts of the audience in the thumbs-up part will apparently have the opposite effect.

NATALYA DEMKINA

Born Natalya Nikolayevna Demkina, in Saransk, western Russia, in 1987, this paranormal talent is able to make medical diagnoses by using "special vision." The "X-ray Girl," as she was nicknamed by the Russian tabloid newspaper, *Pravda*, is apparently able to see organs and tissues inside human bodies and discover medical ailments the person may be suffering from.

Since the age of ten, after an operation to have her appendix removed, Natalya Demkina (also known as Natasha) has been making accurate medical readings in Russia. In her own words: "for a fraction of a second, I see a colorful picture inside the person and then I start to analyze it." Demkina's abilities were tested by doctors at a children's hospital in her hometown, where she was reported to have correctly diagnosed the illnesses of several patients, including one of the doctors.

After using her special vision to examine the patients, sometimes even down to molecular level, Natalya has drawn pictures of what she saw inside their bodies. On one occasion she also corrected a misdiagnosis made by a doctor at the hospital on a female patient who was told she had cancer. When Natalya examined the woman she only saw a "small cyst." Apparently, secondary examination revealed that Natasha had been right and the woman did not have cancer.

After the news of Natalya's incredible ability spread, the story was picked up in 2003 by a local Russian newspaper and television station, and eventually by UK

Saransk

Left **Demkina was born in Saransk, western Russia.**

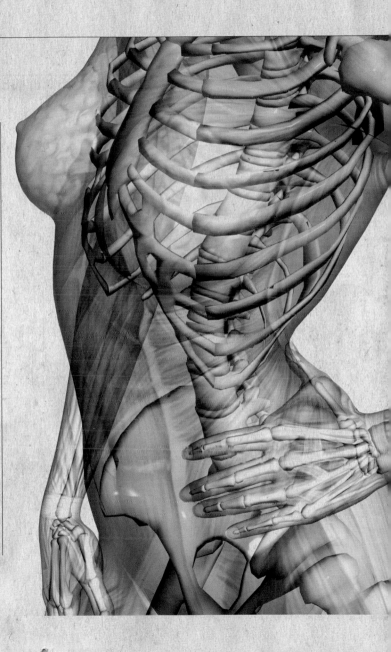

newspaper, *The Sun*. The newspaper brought Natalya to England in January 2004, where she allegedly demonstrated her diagnostic powers successfully on *The Sun* reporter Briony Warden, who had received multiple injuries after being hit by a car the previous October. While in England, Natalya also examined resident medic of the *This Morning* television show, initially making correct identifications of previous medical operations he had undergone, and then stating that the doctor was suffering from various ailments including "gall stones, kidney stones, an enlarged liver, and an enlarged pancreas." Somewhat shaken, the doctor underwent a scan at a local hospital to discover how accurate Natalya's diagnosis had been. He discovered that although the scan did show a possible tumor in his intestines, there were no serious health problems.

NATALYA DEMKINA

The best known and most controversial test performed on Demkina's supernatural powers was that organized by the Discovery Channel in New York in May 2004. The test, which was part of a Discovery Channel documentary entitled *The Girl with X-Ray Eyes*, was carried out by researchers Ray Hyman and Richard Wiseman from the Committee for Skeptical Inquiry (CSI), and Andrew Skolnick of the Commission for Scientific Medicine and Mental Health (CSMMH). The four-hour long investigation involved seven test persons, one of whom was a "normal control subject." Natalya was given seven diagnoses written by doctors and was required to match at least five of these to the corresponding patients in order to prove that her abilities were unusual enough to warrant further testing. In the event Natalya was able to match only four of the seven correctly and thus the researchers concluded that she had failed the test and left it at that.

Acrimonious disputes arose between Natalya and her supporters, who believed she had been unfairly dealt with by the investigators. The research team responded by asking why Natalya had been unable to detect a metal plate inside one subject's head, especially as its outline was visible beneath the person's skull.

The Discovery Channel experiment with Natalya remains controversial to this day and is still the subject of heated debate on internet science and paranormal forums. But there are two points which are worth bearing in mind. Firstly, before the test, Natalya had claimed that she would be "100 percent correct" in her diagnoses, which was obviously not the case. Secondly, she had also agreed to the rules of the experiment, which stated that to pass the test she would have to correctly match at least five of the diagnoses with the corresponding patients. For her complaints to have any validity, they should have been made before the tests began.

After the inconclusive nature of the UK and New York tests, Natalya traveled to Tokyo, Japan, where she underwent experiments with Professor Yoshio Machi, of the Department of Electronics at Tokyo Denki University, who studies claims of unusual human abilities. This time Natalya stipulated beforehand that she

would only be tested under certain conditions, which included that each patient brought with them a medical certificate stating the condition of their health, and that her diagnoses were to be limited to a single specific part of the body—the head, the trunk, or extremities. The teenager also

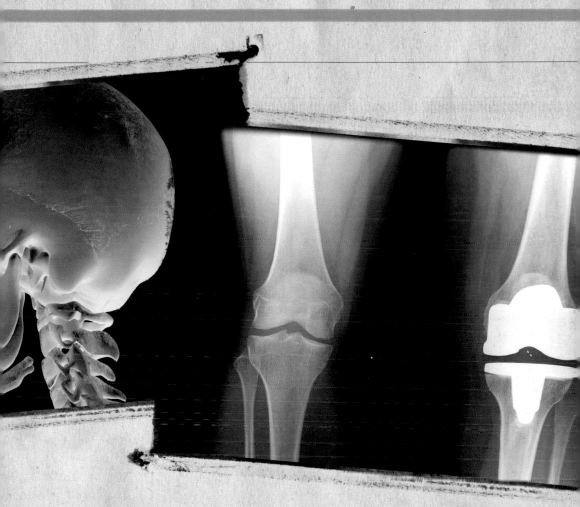

insisted that she was to be told in advance which part of the body she was to examine. According to the newspaper *Pravda*'s website (www.pravda.ru), the tests were successful, with Natalya able to "see" that one of the patients had a prosthetic knee, and another had asymmetrically placed internal organs. She was even able to diagnose the early stages of pregnancy in a female patient.

However, practically all the information we have pertaining to the Tokyo tests comes either from Natalya's own website or from the *Pravda* website. Critics point out that, as with Demkina's tests in

Above **Demkina came to be known as "the X-ray Girl."**

NATALYA DEMKINA

Special Diagnostics of the Person (TSSD), a diagnostic and treatment center for patients in Moscow, where she is in charge of the Office of Energy-Information Diagnostics.

Demkina's role in this office is to diagnose illnesses and supervise their treatment by other healers with unusual abilities. Though still encouraged and courted by the

England, the Tokyo experiments were not performed under strict conditions, nor were they subject to independent review.

Demkina still remains an extremely controversial subject, not least because she has reportedly begun to charge around US$13 for her medical readings, describing the money as donations. Natalya performs between ten and twenty diagnoses per night each weekday, which gives her a salary far above the average monthly income of government workers in her hometown of Saransk. In 2005, Natalya opened the Center of

Right **CT scan of a human abdomen. Demkina informed the resident medic for British TV show *This Morning* that he was suffering from various ailments including "gall stones, kidney stones, an enlarged liver, and an enlarged pancreas," though scans showed he had no serious health problems.**

media, since failing the Discovery Channel tests in 2004, The X-Ray Girl has been all but dismissed by mainstream medicine.

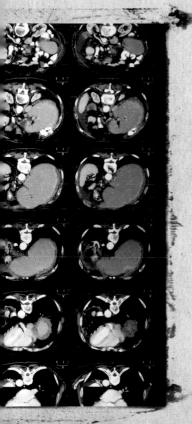

Demkina originally agreed to the experiments in New York because she wanted tangible proof of her alleged abilities: "I just wanted people to acknowledge that this phenomenon exists," she quoted to British newspaper *The Guardian*. However, after testing was complete, Demkina claimed the atmosphere surrounding her experiment was "unfriendly," and the conditions she was instructed to find were "dubious." The television show was choreographed by a professional skeptic association, so perhaps she should have expected their tests to be a little hostile. Conversely, the "successful" Tokyo tests were administered by an academic who writes in support of alternative medicine. At the very least, the case of The X-Ray Girl shows how difficult it is to test paranormal abilities with science. Demkina's supporters and skeptics each argued the other's experiments were faulty, and both groups felt one set of experiments was correct, "proving" their opinions were right all along.

X-RAY VISION

Natalya Demkina's alleged X-ray vision falls into the category of clairvoyant sight, or eyeless vision. Similar claims have been recorded for hundreds of years—from witch trials, to freak shows, modern magicians, and even Cold War intelligence-gathering (when the US and USSR competed for a paranormal advantage).

The question of "testing" such power is a tricky one in situations where scientists are actively seeking the paranormal abilities. For example, the USSR tried to produce measurable data based on biology and the scientific method. The US on the other hand, required psychologists to explore the indeterminate mysteries of the human mind. Using both methods, it is very difficult to "prove" that eyeless vision exists, but also impossible to demonstrate that it doesn't.

DOWSING

Dowsing is the supernatural ability to find hidden objects (often lost valuables), substances (such as underground water, ore deposits, and oil), geographic features (tunnels and caves for example), or sometimes even people. The dowser does not employ scientific apparatus in his or her work but a variety of much simpler tools, most often an A-, Y-, or L-shaped twig or rod (usually known as a divining rod or dowsing rod), but also a pendulum, a map, a photograph, or no equipment at all. Dowsing is a type of *rhabdomancy*, a method of divination using any rod, wand, staff, or stick. The practice is also sometimes known as "water divining," and in the US the term "doodlebugging" is often used to denote dowsing.

Danish dowser Thomas Haulrig uses double L-shaped rods to locate water or high-voltage cables underground.

Nowadays, when the dowser uses two rods, they are often made of copper and formed into an L-shape, though occasionally metal coat hangers are said to work just as well. Formerly, dowsing rods were always of wood, usually a forked hazel branch, though apple, beech, willow, and alder were also used. The modern dowser in search of underground water sources usually holds one rod in each fist and walks around "scanning" the ground until they feel a definite movement of the rods or the rods cross (sometimes they may move suddenly outward). If the dowser is using a forked wooden stick it is most common to feel a downward pull on the stick, although some dowsers feel the stick jerk or writhe in their hands. These movements indicates that the dowser is standing over a water source. The skills of some expert dowsers do not stop at

Above: Map dowsing, also known as remote dowsing, has been described as the highest art form of the dowsing world.

discovering the water, they even claim to be able to estimate its depth, its rate of flow, and its usability as drinking water or for watering crops.

Another form of dowsing is map dowsing, where the device used is usually a pendulum of crystal or metal, which the dowser swings over a map, most often in an attempt to locate oil, minerals, water, or even missing persons. When the pendulum swings around in a circle or back and forth over a particular part of the map, then the dowser knows they have found the target area in which to begin a search.

No one is really sure how dowsing works, or even if it really works at all. One rather vague theory is that all things, both animate and inanimate, possess some kind of energy force which is picked up by the dowser

in the form of vibrations which causes the movement in their stick or rods. Others have suggested that there are electromagnetic or other subtle geological forces at work which the dowser has trained him or herself to pick up on.

Although dowsing is said to date far back into ancient history—there are supposed representations in ancient Egyptian and Chinese art for example—the earliest written accounts of the ability date from the Middle Ages in Europe, when dowsers were employed to locate coal deposits. In fifteenth-century Germany, dowsing was one of the methods used to find metals. Martin Luther (1483–1546), the German theologian who inspired the Protestant Reformation, denounced it as "the work of devil" (which is apparently where the term "water witching" originates). In his 1556 work, *De Re Metallica* ["On the Nature of Metals (Minerals)"] German scholar and scientist Georgius Agricola included an illustration of a German dowser at work and a description of dowsing with a forked twig, although he dismissed the practice himself.

Martin Luther denounced dowsers as practitioners of evil.

A man dowsing for water in the early 1900s.

In a 1959 experiment for the US Navy, dowser Verne L. Cameron (1896–1970) allegedly used his map dowsing ability to locate the entire US submarine fleet in the Pacific Ocean within the space of a few minutes. In the 1960s, the US Army is rumored to have trained soldiers in Vietnam to dowse for unexploded bombs and landmines, and allegedly many lives were saved as a result of their work.

In November of 1990 in Kassel, Germany, a detailed three-day study of 30 dowsers was undertaken by the German Society for the Scientific Investigation of the Parasciences. The three scientists heading the project designed two experiments, the first to test the dowser's ability to detect whether water was flowing in a buried pipe and the second to test the ability of the dowser to locate hidden objects of various materials (including iron, coal, gold, silver, and copper). Although the dowsers were initially confident of a 100 percent success rate, the results produced by the two experiments were unfortunately no better than chance.

Skeptics believe that dowsing, rather than representing some kind of supernatural ability, can be explained by what is known as the "ideomotor effect." Ideomotor actions are unconscious, involuntary muscular movements performed by a person due to suggestion, prior expectations, or preconceptions. The term, "ideomotor action," was introduced as early as 1852 by William B. Carpenter to explain the movements of dowsing rods and pendulums as well as table movement at séances, and the movement of Ouija boards. However, the hundreds of thousands of "successful" dowsers all over the world would undoubtedly disagree with such a prosaic explanation for their powers.

Dowsing became popular in seventeenth-century France with the dowser Baroness de Beausoleil and her husband, a mining expert, journeying across Europe and allegedly locating ore deposits of iron, gold, and silver. The couple established a thriving mineral company, but when their methods for locating metal ores became known they were accused of practicing the "black arts" and imprisoned for the rest of their lives.

It was not until the nineteenth century, with the rise of scientific thought and an increase in religious tolerance, not to mention the appearance of spiritualism, that dowsing came to the attention of the general public. One of the most famous dowsers at this time was English stonemason John Mullins (1838–1894), whose first attempt at the craft saw the rod move so violently that it snapped in two. Mullins was said to be an extremely successful "water diviner," locating over five thousand sources of water in his career.

HOW TO

TEST YOUR DOWSING ABILITIES

1. HOW MANY REAL PEOPLE ARE KNOWN TO HAVE HAD THIS POWER?

Compared to other supernatural abilities, many people have exhibited this power.

2. HOW IS THE POWER ACQUIRED?

Many people are apparently able to acquire the skill through constant practice.

3. WHAT ARE THE EARLY WARNING SIGNS?

Unexplained physical sensations while over underground deposits of water or other substances.

4. HOW DO I KNOW IF I HAVE THE POTENTIAL TO DEVELOP THIS POWER?

If you have the ability to pick up on the vibrations which all living things emit.

5. WHAT MATERIALS WILL I NEED FOR THE TEST?

A forked or L-shaped dowsing rod, or a pendulum.

6. WHAT ARE THE DANGERS ASSOCIATED WITH THIS POWER?

There are none, and you might find some very interesting things in your surroundings.

TEST

MAKE AND USE
A DOWSING ROD

[1] Obtain two 20-inch (0.5-meter) lengths of heavy wire (even coat hangers will work).

5"

[2] Bend the wire into an "L" shape, about 5 inches (12 cm) from one end. The smaller part of the wire is the handle, which you can make more comfortable by slipping pens with the centers taken out (or a few cotton reels glued together) over the wire.

[3] For safety's sake, the long end should be covered in some kind of tape (masking tape will do).

[4] Make another rod in the same way as the first.

[5] Ask a friend to bury a metal object or a container of water in the ground outside just a few inches below the surface. Ask them to make sure they leave no signs that the ground has been disturbed.

[6] Hold the dowsing rods in your hands just above waist level, with the short arm of the L held upright, and the long arm pointing forward. Grip the rods loosely, allowing them to swing freely.

[7] Start walking slowly, mentally asking your dowsing rods to indicate when you are passing over the buried object. Keep aware of the movements of the rods.

[8] When the rods move over a specific spot, usually by crossing over in an X-shape, or swinging outward, stop and find out how successful your dowsing has been.

[9] If you don't succeed with metal rods, try a forked wooden branch, or even a different kind of target. Make sure you keep a record of your various attempts for reference, and don't give up.

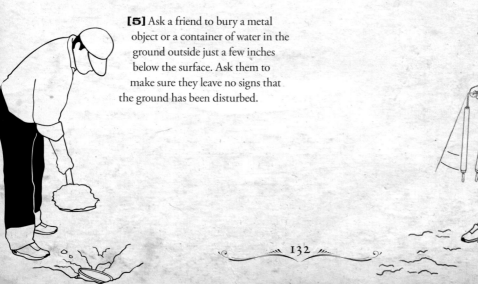

J. RAOUL DEROSIERS

A Canadian businessman named J. Raoul Derosiers allegedly possessed one of the strangest paranormal talents on record—he could, apparently, see deep inside the solid earth. This X-ray vision was at one time known as "water witching," but nowadays is more commonly called water divining or dowsing.

According to the story, Derosiers had often suffered from acute stabbing pains under his lower ribs but, although the attacks were painful, they never lasted long, so for a while he ignored them. In 1940, however, the attacks started to occur more frequently and for much longer durations, persuading him that he needed to visit a doctor. The doctor informed him that he believed the problem was mainly psychological, and would be cured by rest. Accordingly, he prescribed Derosiers sleeping pills, and indeed, this appeared to work for a while.

After he had been taking the pills for about a month, Derosiers

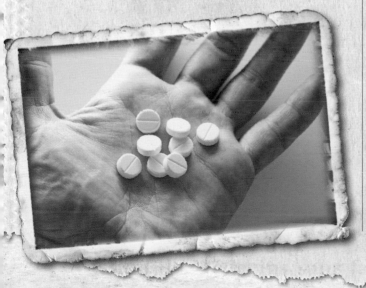

visited a cousin's farm in Québec. The relative complained that lack of water was forcing him out of the cattle business, but although Derosiers sympathized with him, there was nothing he could do. A few months later, on another visit to the farm, the two men were walking across a field behind the barns, when Derosiers got one of his terrible pains in the ribs. As it was happening, he apparently said to his cousin: "Don't ask me why I say this, for I can't explain it—but I feel that I am standing over a stream of underground water… good water. It is seventy feet down and it runs over the top of a layer of

J. RAOUL DEROSIERS

slate three inches thick. Don't drill through that slate or you will lose the water." Three weeks later, the well was drilled in the place where Derosiers had indicated using his "mental X-ray," and to the astonishment of onlookers, an abundant supply of drinkable water was discovered only a foot deeper than he had specified. Not only that, underneath the water was a layer of slate three to four inches in thickness, exactly as Derosiers had predicted.

News of Derosiers and his miraculous "water witching" spread quickly throughout the area and also beyond, and he soon found his supernatural vision very much in demand. It is reported that throughout his career as a dowser, Derosiers chose correct locations for over 600 wells, without a single failure, simply by walking over the land and stopping when he began feeling the stabbing pain in his ribs, or sometimes in the soles of his feet.

In a series of tests of Derosiers' strange ability, skin potential activity (SPA) changes of 100–200 millivolts were recorded for him whenever he walked over a known water vein. In contrast, people without the ability to dowse registered only 10–30 millivolt changes when walking over the area. The details of these fascinating tests, however, which presumably took place in the late 1940s–1950s, appear never to have been published.

If accounts of Derosiers are accurate (sources for the case are slim on the ground and rather sensationalist in nature), then it appears that Derosiers

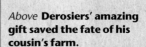

Above **Derosiers' amazing gift saved the fate of his cousin's farm.**

was using his body as a dowsing rod. Apparently, his clients said he never missed. It has been theorized that it may have been the doctor's prescribed sleeping pills which caused some change in Derosiers which facilitated this extraordinary skill. Or perhaps, the case is merely a modern folktale.

Though his X-ray method of detection was bizarre to say the least, Derosiers' ability is not totally unique, there have been, and are still, dowsers who claim similar skills. Celebrated

Right **Bleton, blindfolded and using no apparatus, convinces scientists of his dowsing ability.**

eighteenth-century French dowser, Barthelemy Bleton (his abilities were apparently utilized by Louis XVI and Marie-Antoinette), accidentally discovered his own talents at the age of seven when, after he had carried dinner to a group of workmen, Barthelemy sat down on a large rock for a rest and had a sudden fit. He remained extremely unwell until he was removed from the spot, when he recovered. However, every time he went near the rock his illness returned. His curiosity aroused, a prior from the local monastery ordered the area around the stone to be dug up, revealing a powerful underground spring, which was allegedly still in use at the beginning of the twentieth century.

SCRYING

More popularly known as "Crystal gazing," scrying is a technique of divination. Scrying usually takes the form of gazing at a shiny object—most often a mirror, crystal ball, a stone, or water (though anything which reflects will work), to produce visions which may be of the future, the past, or even the present. Another popular form of scrying is "pendulum scrying," the best-known example of which is when the wedding ring of a pregnant woman is attached to a chain and suspended over the unborn child to determine whether it will be a boy or a girl.

The term "scrying" comes from the Middle English word *descry* , which means "to make out dimly," or "to reveal." It ultimately derives from the Old French *descrier*, "to cry out, to proclaim."

Most researchers agree that by staring at the crystal ball, mirror, or liquid, the scryer enters a trance state. When the scryer enters this state, if he or she is using a crystal ball, there may be a milky clouding of the ball before clear visions appear, which can either have symbolic meaning or show actual people, places, and events. These visions are then interpreted by the scryer, often to give advice or help to the person who has consulted them, or sometimes for the purpose of fortune-telling. Where these visions or messages come from is a matter of some debate. Some researchers

Scrying has been used in many cultures as a means of divining the past, present, and future.

Above: Dr. John Dee and his assistant Edward Kelley making magic together.

them an occult language known as "Enochian" or "Angelical," which according to Dee's journals, was the language God used to create the world, and which was later spoken by Adam to communicate with God and the angels. "Enochian Magic," a system of ceremonial magic based on the evocation and commanding of various spirits, is still used by occultists today.

There is great controversy about the usefulness, and indeed the reality, of scrying. Occultists, and some parapsychologists believe that divination in general accesses some unknown psychic force, or at least taps into the subconscious of the scryer. The crystal or mirror acts to focus the person's psychic energy, but it is generally regarded as not possessing any magic power in itself, rather it is a physical instrument for the prophetic visions the scryer obtains, much akin to the scientist's use of a telescope or a microscope to aid physical vision.

However, skeptics maintain that, if not an outright fraud, then the scryer is probably hallucinating due to sensory deprivation, most often caused by prolonged concentration on a single object. Unfortunately, the reputation of the genuine scryer, if they do actually exist, has been considerably damaged by the numerous money-making fortune-tellers which the newspapers, magazines, and the Internet are now full of.

believe they originate in the unconscious mind of the scryer, while others think they come from angels, demons, disembodied spirits, or even that they are a sign of direct communication with God.

Divination in the form of scrying has a long history. In *Genesis*, Joseph uses his silver drinking chalice for divination, and English writers Chaucer, Spenser, and Shakespeare all refer to the practice. One of the most famous of all scryers was the fascinating and mysterious John Dee (*c.*1527–1608), geographer, astrologer to Queen Elizabeth, and also an Admiralty spy (with the code-number 007, incidentally). In later life Dee became obsessed with the supernatural and in 1582, after years of unsuccessful attempts, he made his first contact with the spirit world using his crystal ball. Later that same year Dee met a 27-year-old scryer named Edward Kelley whom he asked to help him communicate with angels.

Dee and Kelley used a mirror of obsidian (a hard, dark volcanic glass) or a small globe of rock crystal for scrying purposes and on one of their "spiritual conferences," as Dee referred to them, made contact with an angel named "Ave." This angel revealed to

HOW TO

TEST YOUR SCRYING ABILITY

1. HOW MANY PEOPLE ARE KNOWN TO HAVE HAD THIS POWER?

Though many modern "fortune-tellers" claim this power, it is probably not particularly common.

2. HOW IS THE POWER ACQUIRED?

Most people claim to have been born with the scrying ability, though some are able to acquire it though practice.

3. WHAT ARE THE EARLY WARNING SIGNS?

Vivid dreams or visions.

4. HOW DO I KNOW IF I HAVE THE POTENTIAL TO DEVELOP THIS POWER?

The ability to put yourself into a trance, and a vivid imagination, are required for scrying.

5. WHAT MATERIALS WILL I NEED FOR THE TEST?

A bowl of water, a black scrying mirror, a crystal ball, or a pendulum.

6. WHAT ARE THE DANGERS ASSOCIATED WITH THIS POWER?

Beware of becoming obsessed with the supernatural like John Dee (see page 138).

HOW TO

MAKE A SCRYING MIRROR

The easiest way to create a homemade scrying mirror is simply to add some drops of black ink to a bowl of water. This can be used in exactly the same way as you would use a scrying mirror, and has the advantage of being a lot cheaper.

It is generally agreed among scryers that the best scrying mirrors are those made from obsidian. Round mirrors of highly polished black obsidian, which have recently become available at many New Age stores, are thought to be the most effective. Many occultists believe that black obsidian absorbs negative energy and offers protection to the scryer, as well being perfect for displaying prophetic visions.

Another possibility is to use an old mirror (the older the better, according to some scryers), perhaps bought from a flea market. Ideally, the mirror should be round or oval and the frame should be silver (a metal closely linked with the

moon). Do not worry if the mirror is marked or slightly damaged (as long as it is not cracked). The most important thing is that it feels right to you when you hold it in your hands. Alternatively you can use a silver picture frame. All you need to do is remove the protective glass from the frame and insert a mirror in its place. You then have an ideal scrying mirror.

The procedure for making a black scrying mirror is a little more difficult and time-consuming. However, you will find that it's worth the effort. A black mirror is superior to an ordinary mirror for scrying simply because black mirrors reflect less light, so you do not become distracted by the reflected images. Remember—the scryer is not seeking reflections but visions. Follow the steps opposite to make a simple black scrying mirror.

[1] Take an old photo frame and remove the glass covering.

[2] Wipe the glass clean.

[3] Paint one side of the glass with black enamel paint. Oil-based enamels are preferred as they are more durable. It will probably require a few coats before it is completely opaque.

[4] Leave the glass until the paint is completely dry and hardened. This can take two or three days.

[5] When you are sure the paint has dried, carefully remove any hairs, dust, or clinging bits of fiber.

[6] Insert the "mirror" into the frame with the unpainted side facing outward.

[7] You have now created a perfect black scrying mirror.

SCRYING MIRROR TIPS

To prevent the paint getting scratched, you can cover it with a layer of felt or fabric.

The thicker the glass, the more effective your scrying mirror should be.

Black isn't the only option; cobalt blue enamel paint also creates a very good scrying mirror.

Using oil-based gloss enamel paint gets the best results.

* Always be careful when handling glass.

HOW TO

USE A SCRYING MIRROR

[1] Use dim lighting or light a few candles in the room so there are no distracting reflections on the surface of the scrying mirror. This also helps to create the appropriate atmosphere.*

[2] Sit down with both feet in contact with the ground, and make yourself as comfortable and relaxed as you can. This can be achieved by simple deep-breathing exercises or meditation. Bear in mind that scrying should not be undertaken in an anxious state of mind.

[3] If possible, place the scrying mirror at an angle to yourself, to avoid seeing your own reflection.

[4] Look into the mirror and try and let your focus slip beneath the surface, as it were. Do not try and force images to appear.

[5] After a while the scrying surface may appear cloudy, as if early morning mist were creeping across it. It may also seem as if the surface is receding or advancing toward you. These are signs that you are accessing your subconscious.

[6] Soon flashes of images will begin to appear, perhaps unrecognizable at first, but more coherent the longer you sit. Try and make a mental note of these images without breaking concentration.

[7] Wait until the images stop appearing. Take a few deep breaths and look around the room to "ground" yourself again. Make notes of what you saw in a journal.

[8] Put out the candles and turn on the light.

[9] While some people are able to scry at the first attempt, most need to practice the art before obtaining any insightful results.

* Be careful to never fall asleep with candles lit.

HOW TO
DO PENDULUM SCRYING

The most popular form of pendulum scrying is to suspend a crystal from a chain to divine "yes" or "no" answers to simple questions. Consequently, the scryer must first determine which direction indicates a "yes" answer and which will mean a "no." To do this you must think of a question to which the answer is definitely yes, and make a note of which direction the pendulum swings. Repeat the process to establish how to recognize a no answer. When you have done this, you are ready to attempt pendulum scrying.

[1] First get yourself into a relaxed, meditative state. Make sure you are not unduly anxious about the success of your first pendulum scrying experiment.

[2] Hold the chain of your pendulum between your thumb and forefinger and let the pendulum hang down. Do not let the end of the pendulum touch anyone or anything.

[3] Before you begin, make sure your hand and arm are completely still and wait until the crystal has stopped swinging.

[4] Mentally ask a question about something you know you will find the answer to in the next day or two. Examples you could try include sports results, the weather forecast, or even questions about what will happen to you on a specific day of the week. Try and keep the question as clear and simple as you can, with a clear "yes" or "no" answer.

[5] When the pendulum responds with a yes or no answer, make sure you note it down.

[6] When the event you asked about occurs, you can check the pendulum's accuracy by looking at your notes.

ANIMAL ESP

The supposed sensitivity of animals to supernatural phenomena has been recorded for centuries, from their radar-like awareness of approaching natural disasters (see page 151) to pets who possess "psychic" powers, such as sensing the death of their owner even if they are some distance away at the time. Over the last few decades, researchers in the US, Russia, and China have been conducting experiments in an attempt to validate the numerous anecdotal claims of "animal ESP," as it has been nicknamed, though results produced so far have been inconclusive.

One classic story of animal ESP involves Private James Brown of the first North Staffordshire Regiment, UK, who was fighting in the First World War in France, in August 1914. On November 27, Brown received a letter from his wife in London telling him the bad news that Prince, his Irish terrier, had gone missing. Brown, however, was not worried, the dog was with him in the trenches. According to the story, the dog had somehow made his way through the South of England, crossed the English Channel and then walked another 60 miles through war-torn France to his master's front-line position in the trenches at Armentieres. After this incredible feat, Prince was adopted by the regiment and spent the rest of the war with them.

Animals are widely rumored to be particularly sensitive to supernatural phenomena.

Parapsychologists have come up with the term "psi trailing," to describe cases like that of Brown and his dog Prince, where lost or abandoned animals find their way home or manage to locate their owner, sometimes traveling hundreds or even thousands of miles to do so.

Another example of this ability is the well-documented story of Hector, the stowaway dog. On the morning of April 20, 1922, a large black-and-white terrier was seen sniffing around four different ships in the Vancouver docks by a ship's officer called Harold Kildall. The next day, as Kildall's own ship the SS *Hanley* was leaving for Japan he was amazed to find the dog walking about on the deck of the vessel. Three weeks later, when the SS *Hanley* was preparing to unload its cargo of lumber in Yokohama, the dog became agitated as it drew closer to a Dutch merchant ship called the SS *Simaloer*. Some time afterward a boat put out from the Dutch vessel and the dog began barking and leaping up and down excitedly, behaving as if it was about to jump overboard into the sea. As the

boat approached the SS *Hanley* one of its passengers began shouting and waving his arms. This man was Willem H. Mante, second officer of the SS *Simaloer*, and owner of Hector, the black and white terrier, from whom he had become separated at the Vancouver docks.

A book, *Hector the Stowaway Dog*, chronicling this astonishing story was written by Kenneth Dodson in 1958, and was made into a Walt Disney television movie in 1964, re-titled, *The Ballad of Hector the Stowaway Dog: Where the Heck Is Hector?*

Left: Hector the Stowaway Dog became separated from his owner and found him again, sensing his ship from a distance while out at sea.

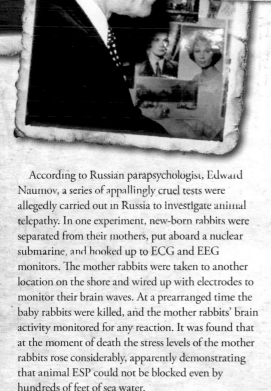

Left: Naumov has claimed that appallingly cruel experiments were carried out in Russia to investigate animal ESP.

According to Russian parapsychologist, Edward Naumov, a series of appallingly cruel tests were allegedly carried out in Russia to investigate animal telepathy. In one experiment, new-born rabbits were separated from their mothers, put aboard a nuclear submarine, and hooked up to ECG and EEG monitors. The mother rabbits were taken to another location on the shore and wired up with electrodes to monitor their brain waves. At a prearranged time the baby rabbits were killed, and the mother rabbits' brain activity monitored for any reaction. It was found that at the moment of death the stress levels of the mother rabbits rose considerably, apparently demonstrating that animal ESP could not be blocked even by hundreds of feet of sea water.

English biochemist and plant physiologist, Rupert Sheldrake, believes that human and animal consciousness extends beyond the brain, and he has come up with the theory of "morphic fields" to explain animal ESP. According to Sheldrake, a morphic field is a field of form, pattern, order, or structure which organizes the fields of living organisms, as well as the forms of crystals and molecules. Every plant and animal has its own group of morphic fields, though Sheldrake believes that personal thoughts, experiences, and memories may not be stored in the brain, but outside in a morphic field. That means any person or animal can obtain information from the memory field —hence ESP.

However, skeptics remain unconvinced of the reality of animal ESP, mainly based on questions of the reliability of witnesses, the lack of corroborative evidence in many cases, and the anecdotal nature of most of the evidence.

HOW TO

TEST ANIMAL ESP

1. HOW MANY ANIMALS ARE KNOWN TO HAVE HAD THIS POWER?

Many animals are said to possess some kind of ESP.

2. HOW IS THE POWER ACQUIRED?

No one knows how this power is acquired.

3. WHAT ARE THE EARLY WARNING SIGNS?

Animals may appear disturbed and behave erratically if something has happened to their owner, even if the animal is separated by some distance from them.

4. HOW DO I KNOW IF MY PET CAN DEVELOP THIS POWER?

Some animals are said to be able to sense danger before humans can, and locate former homes even if they are hundreds of miles away. If your pet has either of these abilities it should be quite evident from their everyday behavior.

5. WHAT MATERIALS WILL I NEED FOR THE TESTS?

Just your pet and some of his or her usual treats.

6. WHAT ARE THE DANGERS ASSOCIATED WITH THIS POWER?

There are none—it's good to make lots of animal friends.

TEST
YOUR PET'S ESP

[4] While you are on your walk, try thinking of something other than your pet, but as soon as you decide to return home, imagine as clearly as you can that you are giving your pet their treat. Make sure you note down the exact time you decided to return home.

[5] When you get back, compare notes with the other person. Does the time you decided to return home from your walk coincide with the time your pet went to the door or window of the house looking for you?

[1] Hold one of your pet's favorite treats under its nose, making as much fuss as possible. However, do not let him/her have any.

[2] Leave the house and go on a short walk, taking the treat with you.

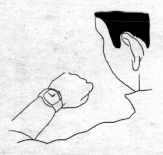

[3] Get a friend to monitor your pet's behavior while you are gone, noting down exactly when the pet looks out of the window or checks the door.

TEST

CAN YOUR PET SENSE DANGER?

[1] Make sure you are in a separate part of the house to your pet.

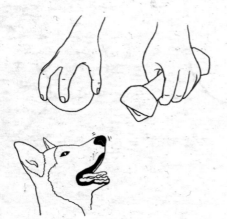

[2] Take out two of your pet's favorite treats. Hold one of them in your hand and imagine that it tastes awful, that the treat is poisonous. Fill your mind with negative images and associate them with this treat.

[3] Visualize your pet being violently ill because of this treat.

[4] Ensure that you do nothing with the other treat.

[5] Make a note of which treat is "the poisonous treat" and return to the room where your pet is.

[6] Place both treats in front of your pet and test whether they have picked up on the negative thoughts you have associated with one of them.

CAN ANIMALS PREDICT EARTHQUAKES?

The ancient city of Helike, once situated on the southern shore of the Gulf of Corinth, roughly 93 miles west of Athens, Greece, was founded in the Early Bronze Age (2600–2300 BCE). One terrible night in the winter of 373 BCE "immense columns of flame" (now known as "earthquake lights") were witnessed in the sky, followed by a massive earthquake and a towering 32-foot (10-meter)-high tsunami wave. The coastal plain was submerged, and as Helike collapsed, the tsunami rushed in and dragged its buildings and its inhabitants back down into the retreating waters. But had this dreadful earthquake been "sensed" by the local animals?

For five days before Eliki disappeared, all the mice and martens and snakes and centipedes and beetles and every other creature of that kind in the town left in a body by the road that leads to Kerynesa. And the people of Eliki seeing this happening were filled with amazement, but were unable to guess the reason. But after the aforesaid creatures had departed, an earthquake occurred in the night; the town collapsed; an immense wave poured over it; and Eliki disappeared, while ten Lacedaemonian [Spartan] vessels which happened to be at anchor close by were destroyed together with the city I speak of.

On the Characteristics of Animals XI.19, Aelian (c.175–235 CE)

CASE STUDY

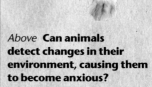

The area around the site of ancient Helike is one of the most seismically active in Europe. In June 1995, an earthquake measuring 6.2 on the Richter scale struck, killing ten people in the nearby town of Aigion, and demolishing a hotel in Eliki, killing sixteen. US astrophysicist, Dr. Steven Soter, collected many descriptions of strange events preceding this quake, which have similarities with ancient accounts of the earthquake which destroyed Helike. Fierce winds were heard when the air was still outside, dogs howled unaccountably, there were subterranean explosions, strange lights in the sky, red glows, and fireballs. Local fishermen witnessed unusually large numbers of octopuses and, the night before the earthquake, numerous dead mice were found on the road, all of which had been run over by cars while trying to make their "escape" into the mountains.

Prior to the February 1960 quake in Agadir, Morocco, which killed 15,000 people (about a third of the city's population), observers claimed that they saw animals, including many dogs, fleeing the town, up to twenty-four hours before the disaster struck. In February 1975, an evacuation warning was issued by seismologists the day before a magnitude 7.3 earthquake struck in Haicheng, China. This warning, the result of the first successful earthquake prediction in history, was based on changes in land elevation and in ground water levels, numerous foreshocks, and widespread reports of peculiar animal behavior, including snakes allegedly coming out of hibernation early.

Such incidents are reminiscent of the behavior of animals in the dreadful Boxing Day 2004 tsunami that struck Sri Lanka, southern India, and Thailand, caused by a huge 9.15 magnitude earthquake in the Indian Ocean. In Sri Lanka, tens of thousands of people lost their lives, wild and

Above **Can animals detect changes in their environment, causing them to become anxious?**

domestic animals seemed to sense what was about to happen and reportedly fled to safety before the tsunami struck. Do all these reports signify that animals possess a "sixth sense" with which they are able to somehow predict a natural disaster?

One experiment which began in 1977 attempted to investigate this theory. The tests, which were sponsored by the US Geological Survey, took place near Palmdale Bulge in the desert northeast of Los Angeles. Kangaroo rats and pocket mice were positioned either in above-

ground cages or in artificial underground burrows where their behavior was tracked by an electronic recorder. Scientists had suspected that the area was seismically active, and in 1979 a number of earthquakes occurred, with the ground shaking for up to twenty seconds in some cases. Disappointingly, however, according to the researchers, the rats and mice had not behaved any differently before these quakes.

If animals can somehow predict earthquakes, how do scientists explain it? Some zoologists have put forward the theory that certain animal species are able to sense subsonic Rayleigh waves (seismic surface waves causing the ground to shake in an elliptical motion) from earthquakes or tsunamis.

Above **Some zoologists claim that animals can sense the waves from earthquakes.**

Other researchers hypothesize that animals may be responding to sound waves that humans cannot hear, or even electromagnetic phenomena. Perhaps animals can detect slight changes in their environment which cause them to behave in an unnatural way? But is this animal ESP?

The evidence for animals predicting earthquakes is controversial and not widely accepted by geologists and seismologists, who point out that in the majority of cases the "facts" are largely anecdotal. Furthermore, scientists believe that accounts of the strange behavior of animals at

times of natural disasters can be ascribed to the "psychological focusing effect;" where people tend to remember strange things happening only after an earthquake or other catastrophic event has taken place. If the disaster had not occurred, the scientists believe, no one would have remembered the strange behavior.

SEE ALSO

Extrasensory perception
Pages 17–21
Animal ESP **Pages 145–150**

MIND OVER MATTER

The powers grouped under this heading involve the ability of the bearer to manipulate physical matter using the strength of the mind. Uri Geller is a famous example of someone reputed to possess this ability, and he has often entertained audiences with his spoon-bending tricks.

PSYCHOKINESIS

Psychokinesis, commonly abbreviated to "PK," is the ability of the human mind to affect physical objects without the use of any known physical force. Popularly known as "mind over matter," PK encompasses "supernatural" abilities such as the various "materialization" phenomena associated with spiritualist séances (see psychic mediumship, pages 67–72), spoon-bending, and "poltergeist" phenomena (which includes the unexplained movement of objects, electrical disturbances, and spontaneous fires). Two broad types of PK have been identified by parapsychologists—phenomena which occur on a "macro" scale, where the effects are obvious to the naked eye, for example the moving of heavy objects; and a "micro" scale, where the effects are too small to be observable to the naked eye. In cases of micro PK, the existence of the ability can only be demonstrated by scientific measuring devices or statistical tests such as those utilizing random number generators.

Occurrences of what may be interpreted as PK have been recorded since ancient times, for example many of the powers attributed to the Greek gods in the writings of Homer; and in the Bible, where there are numerous instances of levitation, miraculous healings, and "apports."

In 1890, Russian psychical researcher Alexander Aksakof (1832–1903) coined the term "telekinesis"

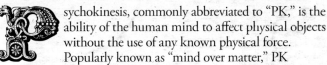

Alexander Aksakof, Russian spiritualist and distinguished psychical researcher.

Left: J. B. Rhine, Psychic researcher.
Above: Random event generator (REG) developed for PK studies by Helmut Schmidt.

(literally "distant movement") for the apparent human ability to move matter at a distance through non-physical means. In 1914, American author and head of the publishers Houghton, Mifflin & Co., Henry Holt (1840–1926) introduced the term "psychokinesis" in his book, *On the Cosmic Relations*. However, the word did not catch on until it was adopted by Joseph Banks Rhine at Duke University in North Carolina in 1934.

One of Rhine's many studies to test for PK involved experiments to determine if a subject could influence the outcome of falling dice. To eliminate unconscious human influence, Rhine used special dice-throwing machines to test students' power to influence the way the dice fell, with his results often well above chance. However, Rhine has often been criticized for the lax conditions of his tests, and also for the failure of other researchers carrying out his experiments to replicate his amazing results.

Rhine's use of technology to test for PK was further developed in the 1960s by physicist Dr. Helmut Schmidt of the Mind-Science Foundation in San Antonio, Texas, who utilized electronic random event generators (REGs). Schmidt based one of his tests on the subject's ability to affect the unpredictability of radioactive decay; if they were successful then the decay would no longer be random. Another, rather simpler, test devised by Schmidt was to ask students to predict which one of four lights would be switched on by the random event generator. The success rate in both of these experiments was apparently much higher than that allowed by chance.

Probably the most famous of all practitioners of PK is Israeli-born psychic, Uri Geller. Geller rose to prominence during the 1970s mainly on TV for his mental bending (of spoons and door keys) and other rather sensational PK abilities, such as causing the broken watches of television viewers to start up again. Geller's abilities also underwent scientific testing. In 1973 and 1974 at the

Naval Surface Weapons Center in Silver Spring, Maryland, Eldon Byrd, a scientist with a keen interest in the paranormal, gave Geller a five-inch (13-cm) long piece of nitinol wire. After a few moments stroking the ends of the material Geller managed to permanently change its shape, a feat normally requiring extremely high temperatures to achieve. Trickery was suspected by skeptical researcher, Martin Gardner, but never proven. More controversially, Geller claimed that he used his psychic powers to bring London's Big Ben clock to a stop in 1989 and 1997, though experts claimed this was caused mainly by unusually high temperatures.

Naturally, Geller has a host of detractors, notably the magician and skeptic James Randi, who insists that Geller, rather than possessing any "psychic powers," utilizes sophisticated stage magician's trickery to achieve his often spectacular results. Gerald Fleming

Above: Uri Geller claims his feats are the result of paranormal powers given to him by extraterrestrials..

has also offered £250,000 (US$360,000) to Uri Geller if he can make a spoon bend "paranormally" under controlled conditions, a challenge Geller has so far refused to take up.

One difficulty in accepting the reality of PK is that although scientists have been investigating it since the mid-nineteenth century, we seem to be no further on in our understanding of this supernatural power. We also have no irrefutable scientific proof of its existence. Why is this? Scientists would argue that for PK to exist it would have to violate many well-established laws of physics. Furthermore, as with all paranormal powers, critics point out that PK has not produced reliable repeatable demonstrations in laboratories.

POLTERGEIST

The German word "poltergeist" roughly translates as "noisy spirit" or "noisy ghost." Although we generally associate the poltergeist with ghosts and haunted houses, poltergeist cases usually involve many of the phenomena attributed to people claiming to possess psychic powers. Parapsychologists often refer to poltergeist phenomena using the rather unwieldy term "recurrent spontaneous psychokinesis" (RSPK).

Common characteristics of the poltergeist include: the movement and hurling around of inanimate objects; the opening and closing of doors and windows; unexplained noises such as voices, moans, screams, explosions, crashes, raps, thumps, scratches, knocks on floors, doors, and walls, and heavy footsteps; bed-shaking; the breaking of household objects such as crockery; the destruction of garments; the throwing of stones, rocks, and dirt; bad smells; mysterious fires; the appearance of pools of water on floors; the malfunctioning of electrical equipment; telephone ringing; the unexplained appearance of objects ("apports"), apparitions; and even physical assault. Stone throwing is very often the first sign of poltergeist activity, with the houses of victims allegedly bombarded by stones and bricks sometimes for days (or even weeks) before any other kind of unusual phenomenon occurs.

THE POLTERGEIST IN HISTORY

Poltergeist-like phenomena have been recorded throughout history, over a large cross-section of cultures and have generally exhibited similar characteristics. First-century Jewish historian, Josephus, describes a "possession" that would nowadays be attributed to poltergeist activity. Jacob Grimm, one of the brothers Grimm, writing in his *Deutsche Mythologie*, describes a number of cases including one from Bingen-am-Rhein dated to 355 CE, where

Left **Skeptics propose poltergeist activity may have a physical explanation—static electricity, electromagnetic fields, and/or ionized air.**

Above **A ripped sweater was the outcome of a physical assault from the Enfield poltergeist.**

stones were thrown, people were pulled out of bed, and raps and loud noises were heard. Writing in his *Itinerarium Cambriae* (1191 CE), of his tour of Wales, clergyman and chronicler, Giraldus Cambrensis describes an incident at a house in Pembrokeshire where "unclean spirits" threw dirt and other objects, clothes were ripped and torn, and the "spirit" even spoke of the various secrets of people present at the time of the occurrence. Medieval chronicles are also full of such incidents.

The problem, however, with such accounts of poltergeist cases is that their sources were not written as "history" as such; medieval chronicles include many signs, wonders, and miracles that were not records of "true" happenings.

One of the most famous poltergeist cases of the last few centuries is the "Tedworth Drummer" of England in 1661. A drum which belonged to an imprisoned beggar apparently played on its own, accompanied by various other phenomena such as the hurling about of chairs, beds with servants sleeping in them being lifted up, and loud

scratching noises. A series of bizarre and frightening incidents which allegedly took place on a Tennessee farm in 1817 has become known as the "Bell witch haunting." The Bell Witch herself was thought by many to be the spirit of Kate Batts, a former neighbor of John Bell, owner of the farm where the disturbances took place, and who had apparently been involved in a dispute with him over land. The phenomena included apparitions of strange animals, whistling, disembodied voices, loud laughing and singing, and vicious physical assaults on people at the farm, which are claimed by some to have resulted in the death of John Bell.

THE ENFIELD AND MACKENZIE POLTERGEIST CASES

Two interesting modern poltergeist cases are the "Enfield poltergeist" and the "Mackenzie poltergeist." The former took place in 1977, in a north London council house, and the phenomena included furniture moving by itself, knockings on the walls, spontaneous fires, pools of water appearing on the floor, cold breezes, physical assaults, the appearance of graffiti, equipment malfunction and failure, and various items being thrown around the house.

The Mackenzie poltergeist case began in 1999 in Greyfriars Kirkyard, Edinburgh. The events were allegedly triggered by a homeless man spending the night in a mausoleum belonging to Sir George Mackenzie, who died in 1691, and was known during his lifetime for his bloody persecution of the

Covenanters, a powerful Scottish Presbyterian movement. The homeless man accidentally caused some damage to Mackenzie's coffin and was subsequently witnessed running and screaming in terror from the site, to be found later in a state of delirium by police. Since that night, strange phenomena have been experienced in the kirkyard and the surrounding area. Neighboring houses were plagued by objects flying around the rooms and crockery smashing, while visitors to the site itself experienced feelings of extreme heat or cold, suffered cuts and bruises from an unknown assailant, had their throats squeezed, coats tugged violently, and were, on occasion, even knocked unconscious by an invisible force. Two subsequent exorcisms of the area failed to halt the phenomena.

EXPLANATIONS FOR THE POLTERGEIST

Parapsychologists have struggled for years to explain the poltergeist phenomenon. Aside from accusations of hoax and exaggeration—explanations which certainly apply to a large percentage of poltergeist cases—the most popular theory is that the "poltergeist" is caused unwittingly by a human agent, usually a teenage girl. Some researchers believe that a troubled adolescent unconsciously manipulates objects using psychokinesis. However, there are also a number of poltergeist cases where the people involved have no psychological problems at all, and where there are no adolescents in the household. How can we explain these? A further point is that there are millions of troubled teenagers all over the world, but they do not cause poltergeist activity to occur.

Other researchers have suggested that "spirit entities" are responsible for the phenomena (perhaps feeding off the power generated by suitably disturbed teenagers). But the very nature of these hypothetical "spirits" means that scientifically they cannot be investigated, though there are interesting tape recordings of a "spirit voice" from the Enfield poltergeist case. However, if accounts of the more extreme occurrences alleged to be caused by poltergeist activity are themselves exaggerated, or even completely unreliable, which is entirely possible in older cases, then no further explanation is required.

More down to earth phenomena are often the cause of what appears to be a poltergeist disturbance. Electromagnetic interference (EMI) has been found to be the explanation of at least one supposed poltergeist investigated by Midlands (UK) investigation group, Parasearch, and there is an increasing amount of evidence to show that it could explain many more cases.

HOW TO

TEST PSYCHOKINESIS

1. HOW MANY PEOPLE ARE KNOWN TO HAVE HAD THIS POWER?

Many physical mediums claimed this power during the heyday of spiritualism in the late nineteenth century. A number of modern-day psychics, including Matthew Manning and Uri Geller, have also allegedly demonstrated this ability.

2. HOW IS THE POWER ACQUIRED?

This power can appear spontaneously or may be hereditary, as in the case of Russian psychic Nina Kulagina, who believed she had inherited her powers from her mother (see page 165).

8. WHAT ARE THE EARLY WARNING SIGNS?

Sometimes poltergeist-like activity may occur in the homes of people allegedly possessing PK; some researchers have suggested this activity is akin to uncontrolled PK.

4. HOW DO I KNOW IF I HAVE THE POTENTIAL TO DEVELOP THIS POWER?

If you have the ability to affect physical objects by thought alone, then you already have this skill and can learn to control it and use it to your advantage.

5. WHAT MATERIALS WILL I NEED FOR THE TESTS?

Internet versions of random number generators (RNGs), a spoon and a glass surface for the Spoon on the Glass Test.

6. WHAT ARE THE DANGERS ASSOCIATED WITH THIS POWER?

There is a danger of becoming exhausted from too much mental effort. Make sure you take breaks between experiments.

RANDOM NUMBER GENERATOR

It is now possible to test for PK using Internet-based versions of random number generators (RNGs), the purpose of which is to randomly generate zeroes and ones. Over a period of time the average between the number of zeros and ones generated by the machine should be 50/50. To take the test you must attempt to mentally influence how many number ones the computer generates by focusing hard on the number one. The purpose is to record how far the results of the RNG vary from the expected statistical 50/50 average. Hypothetically the further the results are from 50/50, the more apparent influence you have had on the RNG.

SPOON ON THE GLASS TEST

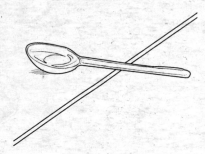

[4] Move your fingers away from the spoon and visualize the spoon moving back upward to its original position. Repeat this process several times.

[5] With enough practice and concentration, the repeated movement of your fingers over the spoon will cause it to rock up and down, and eventually fall off the glass.

[1] Balance an ordinary metal spoon carefully on the side of a glass surface, such as a coffee table.

[2] Concentrate on your fingertips and imagine a strong force field around them. Imagine this force field becoming more powerful the more you concentrate on it.

[3] Place your fingertips near the edge of the spoon handle, being careful not to allow them to come into contact with it. Visualize your fingertips pushing against the spoon causing it to tilt downward slightly.

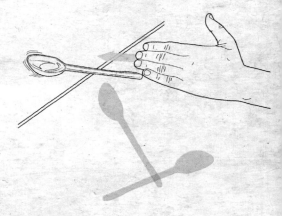

NINA KULAGINA

From the late 1960s to 1990, Russian "psychic," Nina Kulagina, displayed an apparently impressive range of psychic powers, particularly psychokinesis, and was tested and supposedly found to be genuine by respected Russian scientists. She was also filmed using her abilities many times. However, she remains a controversial figure and her demonstrations of psychic ability have received criticism from skeptics who believe the films and experiments show clever trickery rather than paranormal powers.

Kulagina claimed that she had always been aware of her "psychic powers." On one occasion when she was in a particularly angry mood, she was walking toward a cupboard in her apartment when a jug in the cupboard suddenly moved to the edge of the shelf, fell, and smashed to pieces on the floor. After this incident, changes began to take place in her apartment. Lights went on and off; objects became animated and seemed to be attracted to her. It was as if there was a poltergeist in the house, except that Kulagina was convinced that the "psychic power" was coming from her and discovered that, if she tried, she could control it.

One of Kulagina's abilities involved her sitting at a table and staring at a small object, such as a matchbox or a wineglass, and making it move without touching it.

Apparently her powers did not come straight away: hours of preparation would often be needed, which, as skeptics have pointed out, does not favor the setting up of strictly supervised demonstrations. In order for her powers to function, Kulagina claimed she had to clear all other thoughts from her head, and told investigators that when her concentration was successful, there was a sharp pain in her spine, and her eyesight blurred. Apparently she practiced hard, focusing her powers, and was soon able to move matchsticks, fountain pens, and compass needles.

Stories of Kulagina's amazing abilities began to reach the West through the international wire services in the spring of 1968.

NINA KULAGINA

In the same year, films of Kulagina moving objects, ostensibly using only her mind, were shown at the first Moscow International Conference on Parapsychology, and were also seen by some Western scientists. Western investigators were briefly permitted to meet Russian mediums, witness Nina Kulagina for themselves, and verify the reports of her PK abilities made by Soviet scientists. In 1970 William A. McGary, one of a group from the United States investigating psychic phenomena in Russia, described a session in which Kulagina caused several small objects, including a wedding ring and the top of a condiment bottle to move across a dining-room table.

Another of the American investigators, Gaither Pratt, of the University of Virginia, stated that the objects which Kulagina could move varied widely in material, shape, and weight, and when they moved they generally progressed in a slow, steady fashion. Only occasionally did the objects which Kulagina "controlled" move in fits and starts. It is reported that a number of precautions were taken to make sure that Kulagina was not using a concealed magnet or threads, and films were taken of the experiments that seem to confirm that no known force could explain the movements. Unfortunately, it is not known how thoroughly Kulagina was checked before the experiment.

In one test filmed in Moscow, set up by a group of well-known physicists, several non-magnetic objects including matches were placed inside a large Plexiglas cube. The cube was used to prevent the use of drafts of air, threads, or wires—methods long suggested by skeptics as the means by which Kulagina performed her "tricks." Her hands moved a few inches from the Plexiglas cover and the objects danced from side to side in the container. In another filmed experiment, a ping-pong ball is seen levitating and hovering in the air for a few seconds, before falling back onto the table. In yet another she

Left **Kulagina took part in many controlled experiments proving her extraordinary gift.**

is shown both indoors and outside in a garden, where objects close to her spin around or slide in different directions.

Unfortunately the films are so grainy and unclear that it is often difficult to make out exactly what is happening, and again the background information to the experiment—location, precautions taken, persons present etc.—is not given. Where are the reports of these amazing tests?

The most unusual test of all took place in a Leningrad laboratory on 10 March, 1970. Satisfied that Kulagina had the ability to move inanimate objects, scientists were curious to know whether Kulagina's abilities extended to cells, tissues, and organs. In one experiment Kulagina attempted to use her energy to stop the beating of a frog's heart and then re-activate it. She focused intently on the heart and summoned all her powers. First she made it beat faster—then slower, and, using intense will power, she stopped it. Apparently she could also use her power to disrupt human heart beats—on one occasion giving a hostile Leningrad psychiatrist a frightening first-hand experience of her talents.

Despite the lack of concrete evidence for trickery in the case of Nina Kulagina, skeptics still believe her spectacular abilities to be entirely fraudulent or at least greatly exaggerated by Soviet authorities, probably to be used as propaganda in their Cold-War era psychological battles with the US. Indeed the lack of publication of the incredible experiments with Kulagina and other Russian psychics in scientific journals has persuaded some researchers that the experiments never occurred at all, or at least not as described in the popular press.

According to popular accounts, Kulagina's continued use of her supernatural abilities led to a strain on her health culminating, in the late 1970s, in a near-fatal heart attack. Her doctors recommended that she drastically reduce her workload, though she kept up some lab work until she died in 1990, around the time of the death of the Soviet Union itself.

SEE ALSO

Poltergeist **Pages 160–162**
Psychokinesis **Pages 157–164**

PSYCHIC HEALING

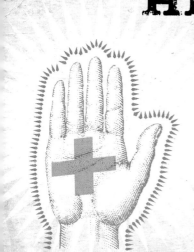

Psychic healing refers to a process during which beneficial biochemical changes are said to take place without conventional medical treatment. This chapter will concentrate on the most controversial aspect of psychic healing—psychic surgery. In this procedure a "psychic doctor" or "psychic surgeon" performs a painless operation without the use of anesthetics or antiseptics. The operation usually involves the surgeon making an "incision" using only his bare hands, and appearing to remove tissue from the patient's body. The wound then heals spontaneously and the patient makes an apparent recovery.

Above: Psychic surgeon Tony Agpaoa.
Left: Brazilian psychic surgeon Edivaldo Silva.

Psychic surgery first appeared in the spiritualist communities of the Philippines and Brazil in the 1940s and 1950s. Even today, thousands of sick people, many beyond the help of conventional medical science, travel to the Philippines in search of a miracle cure. Psychic surgery has become big business there, and in Manila alone there are now hundreds of practicing "surgeons," a large number of whom work out of hotels. The best known of the Filipino psychic surgeons, Tony Agpaoa (1939–1982), began as a young pupil of the psychic healer Eleuterio Terte. In 1967, Agpaoa was indicted for fraud in the United States; nevertheless, by the early 1970s, he had become extremely wealthy as a result of his "psychic operations." However, in 1973, Agpaoa was exposed by an Italian film crew who discovered that the so-called renal stones he apparently took from

Caught out–Agpaoa pretended to remove kidney stones from a patient which were in fact pieces of pumice stone.

During the 1950s, several psychic surgeons rose to prominence in Brazil, most notably Arigó (José Pedro de Freitas, see page 174). Many of these Brazilian healers were associated with spiritism, a religious movement founded in 1857 by Hippolyte Leon Denizard Rivail, better known as Allen Kardec.

It was fairly common in Brazil in the 1950s for psychic surgeons to claim that they were performing their operations as channels for spirits of deceased medical doctors. The death of Arigó in 1971 did not mean the end of his supposed spirit guide, the German doctor, Dr. Fritz. Soon other Brazilian psychic surgeons claimed to be channeling the doctor, including Oscar and Edivaldo Wilde, and a gynecologist from Recife, called Edson Queiroz. The Wilde brothers both died violently in car crashes, while Queiroz was stabbed to death in 1991. Currently, Rubens Farias Jr., a former São Paulo engineer and computer programmer, claims to be the channel for the spirit of Dr. Fritz, who has chillingly predicted a violent death for Farias.

a patient's body were actually pieces of pumice. In his book *Flim-Flam!* James Randi notes that when Agpaoa had to have his own appendix removed he went to a San Francisco hospital for the operation, rather than a psychic surgeon in the Philippines.

Another healer from the Philippines is Alex L. Orbito, apparently the "world's greatest psychic surgeon." Orbito is a full-time medium and spiritual healer who has attracted a great deal of media attention due to the famous patients he has treated, who have included Shirley MacLaine and Saudi royalty.

In March 1984, US comedian Andy Kaufman traveled to the Philippines for a six-week course of psychic surgery after being diagnosed with a rare lung cancer. The surgeon, Jun Labo, performed the operation, and claimed that he had removed large cancerous tumors from Kaufman's body. On May 16, 1984, Kaufman died from renal failure as a consequence of a metastatic lung cancer.

What actually happens during psychic surgery varies from one practitioner to another. Generally however, the surgeon undertakes the procedure with his bare hands or extremely basic medical instruments and leaves little if any trace of the skin having been broken. The "surgery" involves the practitioner pressing the tips of his fingers against the patient's skin over the area to be treated, the skin is then penetrated and blood is seen to pour out of the incision. The practitioner then "removes" organic matter from the body, shows it to the patient, and then cleans the area. During the

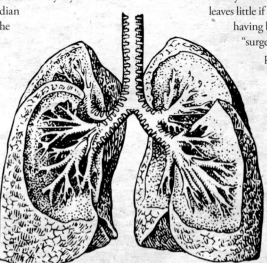

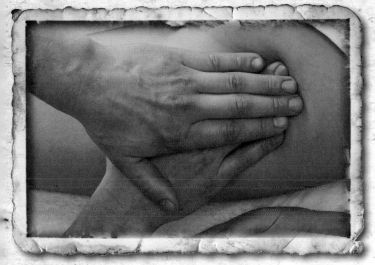

Above: Psychic surgery has been condemned in most countries as a form of medical fraud.

operation the patient feels no pain and there is no trace of wounding or scarring on their skin.

Unsurprisingly, most of today's medical profession considers psychic surgery a complete fraud, an irresponsible practice giving false hope to those suffering from fatal diseases. Debunkers, such as stage conjuror and skeptic, James Randi, contest that in most cases psychic surgeons never pierce the patient's skin at all, but pinch or roll it back over the area to be operated on, place their hand under the roll of skin and "remove" a piece of bloody animal tissue concealed in their clenched fist, or perhaps under the operating table. In many cases of psychic surgery, the blood seen to be coming from the patient's wound was found to be animal blood which the practitioner had squirted from a handheld balloon. Sometimes, mainly in countries where there is a widespread belief in evil spirits, foreign objects will be produced from the patient's body by the surgeon, who claims that they were placed there by evil spirits.

In 1975, the US Federal Trade Commission condemned psychic surgery, calling it a "total hoax,"

and in 1990, the American Cancer Society stated that they found no evidence that "psychic surgery" resulted in "objective benefit in the treatment of any medical condition." Two psychic surgeons who testified before the Federal Trade Commission stated that in most psychic surgery the organic matter removed from the patient's body by the practitioner consists of animal tissue and clotted blood.

The greatest danger of psychic surgery lies in the fact that the patient's belief in its alleged benefits may prevent them from seeking out possibly life-saving medical care, perhaps with fatal consequences. However, although the evidence would suggest that psychic surgery is for the most part sleight-of-hand trickery, there is no doubt that many patients undergoing the procedure (a number of those treated by Arigó for example), appear to have benefited from the treatment. Nevertheless, this is probably best interpreted as a placebo effect, where the power of suggestion played a major part in the apparent success of the "operation."

HOW TO

TEST FOR PSYCHIC HEALING

1. HOW MANY PEOPLE ARE KNOWN TO HAVE HAD THIS POWER?

Very few outside of the Philippines and Brazil.

2. HOW IS THE POWER ACQUIRED?

Many psychic surgeons (including Arigó) claimed they obtained their power from spirits working through them.

3. WHAT ARE THE EARLY WARNING SIGNS?

Feeling your body being "taken over" by something you have no or minimal control over.

4. HOW DO I KNOW IF I HAVE THE POTENTIAL TO DEVELOP THIS POWER?

You either have the power or you don't.

5. WHAT MATERIALS WILL I NEED?

None.

6. WHAT ARE THE DANGERS ASSOCIATED WITH THIS POWER?

There are many dangers associated with the alleged possession of this power. The greatest of these lies in the fact that the patient's belief in its alleged benefits may prevent them from seeking life-saving medical care, with possibly fatal consequences.

TEST

TEST A PSYCHIC SURGEON

You should not attempt to try anything associated with the alleged power of psychic surgery. The following is a test which has been carried out on psychic surgeons in the past.

[1] The surgeon must allow you to walk around the operating table/couch when he/she is working.

[2] You must be allowed to check under and around the table for hidden medical instruments/props.

[3] The surgeon must show you his/her empty hands before he touches the client. Without touching anything, he/she must then start the treatment.

[4] The surgery should be filmed from the front, back, above, and sides.

[5] The resulting film of the operation should be examined by medical doctors for any signs of fakery on the part of the surgeon.

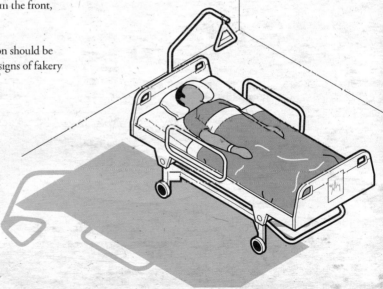

JOSÉ ARIGÓ

One of the most famous psychic surgeons was a poorly educated ex-miner known as Arigó (José Pedro de Freitas), who was born in 1921 in the state of Minas Gerais, Brazil. Arigó came from a poor family, and left school at 14 to begin work in the local mines. When he was 30, Arigó began suffering from depression, fierce headaches, nightmares, sleep-walking, and

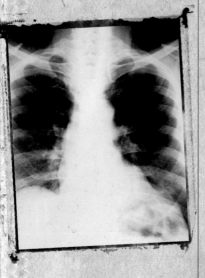

Left **Arigó supposedly removed a cancerous tumor from Brazilian senator, Bittencourt, using a kitchen knife.**

hallucinations. Unable to get any relief from the town doctors, the distraught young man went to a local spiritualist named Olivera, who prayed for him and told him that the cause of the problem was a spirit attempting to work through him. One dramatic event was to convince Arigó of the truth of this statement.

In 1950, state senator Bittencourt invited Arigó, along with some other miners, to attend a rally in the city of Belo Horizonte. Arigó was staying at the same hotel as the senator, who was suffering from a cancerous tumor which required immediate treatment. The senator was intending to travel to

Above **José Arigó, psychic surgeon, on trial in 1964.**

the US to undergo surgery after the rally. That night Arigó entered Bittencourt's room apparently in a state of trance, carrying a razor. The senator passed out only to awake the next morning to find his pajama top slashed, blood on his chest and a neat incision in his ribcage. In a state of profound shock the senator went to find Arigó who remembered nothing of

the incident but helped the dazed man to a taxi which took him to his physician. After taking several X-rays, senator Bittencourt's doctor informed him that the tumor had inexplicably disappeared.

Overwhelmed by his seemingly miraculous cure, Bittencourt started talking about it to his friends and associates and even included it in his political speeches, thus leading to instant fame for Arigó.

Another spectacular case occurred some time in 1956. Arigó and his family were gathered around the bed of a female relative dying from cancer of the uterus. With the priest about to administer the last rites Arigó suddenly ran out of the room into the kitchen, grabbed a knife and came back and thrust it swiftly into the woman's vagina. Twisting the knife around for a few seconds he rapidly extracted the bloody tumor, which he threw, together with the kitchen knife, into the sink. He then collapsed, and subsequently stated that he could remember nothing of the operation. The understandably stunned relatives immediately called a doctor, who confirmed

that Arigó had indeed removed a tumor from the woman, without apparent pain or haemorrhaging. The relative soon recovered completely from the disease.

Arigó claimed that he performed his operations while in a trance state possessed by (or channeling) the spirit of a German doctor called "Dr. Adolphus Fritz," who had apparently died in 1918, during the First World War. This was the spirit that Olivera had said was trying to work through him, and after Arigó began his work as a psychic surgeon his severe headaches stopped and only returned when he later

decided temporarily to discontinue his surgery.

To perform his surgeries, Arigó opened a small clinic in his hometown of Congonhas do Campo, where he would carry out his swift operations free of charge. He possessed no medical knowledge whatsoever, worked in unsanitary conditions, and used

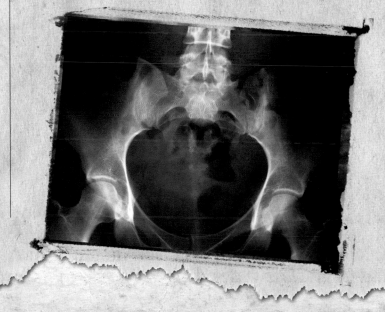

JOSÉ ARIGÓ

only his hands, a rusty knife or occasionally a pair of scissors; his only concession to cleanliness was to wipe his knife on his shirt before and after surgery. Despite these dangerous conditions he allegedly performed a million successful operations over a twenty-year period, regularly treating hundreds of people a day in his surgery. During the operations there would be little bleeding and the patients would feel no pain. There was no need for stitches and wounds would heal remarkably fast; there is also no record of a patient ever having become infected, despite the unsterile conditions.

Unfortunately, the publicity and fame which Arigó's abilities attracted brought him the unwanted attention of the Brazilian government, and he was imprisoned in 1957 for practicing medicine without a license, and again in 1964 on charges connected with witchcraft.

In early January 1971, Arigó began telling his friends and associates, including former President of Brazil, Kubitschek, that they would not see him again, as he would soon die a violent death. A few days later on January 11, he was killed in a car crash. Arigó's hometown of Congonhas do Campo reportedly came to a standstill at the tragic news, flags flew at half mast, and the mayor declared two days of mourning for the great healer.

The evidence, in the form of thousands of testimonies by patients and doctors, photographs

Above **There are no records of any patients becoming infected after seeing Arigó.**

Left **Arigó performed his procedures in extremely unhygienic conditions.**

and movie films, is certainly impressive in the case of Arigó. However, considering that most, if not all, psychic surgery has been shown to be fake, could Arigó have been any different? Many researchers, including James Randi, think not. They believe that Arigó's psychic operations were a complete fraud, and that the wily Brazilian accomplished his "miracles" by relatively basic conjuring tricks, combined with the willingness of his patients to believe he was blessed with some kind of divine healing power. Nevertheless, even if his healing abilities were faked, he was still able in some way to remove all sense of fear and pain from his patients, and to affect their minds in an extremely powerful way. On one occasion, when Arigó was shown a film of himself operating, he fainted. When asked for his own explanation of this incredible ability his reply was disarmingly straightforward: "I simply listen to a voice in my right ear and repeat whatever it says. It is always right."

SEE ALSO

Psychic Mediumship **Pages 67–72**

Channeling **Pages 77–81**

Below **A fatal car accident killed the psychic surgeon in 1971.**

PYROKINESIS

he word "pyrokinesis" derives from the Greek words *pûr* ("fire, lightning") and *kinesis* ("motion"), and refers to the power to create and/or control fire with the mind. As it involves the direct action of mind over material objects, it is considered part of psychokinesis. "Pyrokinesis" was first used to describe a supernatural ability by horror writer Stephen King in his 1980 novel, *Firestarter*. The ability to control fire is found frequently in horror and science fiction books and television shows. Examples include the *Marvel Comics* characters Human Torch and Pyro, *The X-Files* episode "Fire," and the *Fringe* episode "The Road Not Taken."

Stories of fires caused by persons apparently using their mind alone go back at least as far as the nineteenth century—and further if we include poltergeist cases where outbreaks of fire have been attributed to certain individuals in the house. Charles Fort (1874–1932), pioneer investigator of strange phenomena, collected a number of early cases of pyrokinesis (see page 184). In October 1886, a 12-year-old boy named Willie Brough, of Turlock, Madison County, California, was accused of setting things alight "by his glance," and was expelled from Turlock School after five unexplained fires had started in his presence. His parents thought him possessed by the devil and sent

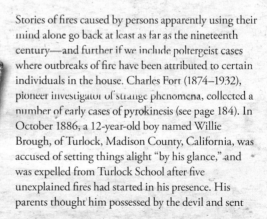

Stories of people possessing the power of pyrokinesis are popular subjects of television and film.

him away (evoking shades of the Stephen King story *Carrie*). At a farmhouse in Bridgewater, Scotland, in May 1878, fires started with no apparent cause. Loud raps were heard and household items such as dishes and loaves of bread moved about. After a police investigation, a servant girl, Ann Kidner, aged 12, was arrested and accused of tossing lighted matches, but was released by the magistrate because of insufficient evidence.

Another case occurred in 1882, in Paw Paw, Michigan, where a 24-year-old man named A. William Underwood, had to take great care whenever he breathed, so as to avoid causing fires. A Dr. L. C. Woodman ran some tests on Underwood, and afterward informed the *Michigan Medical News*:

Charles Dawes was an American banker and politician.

> He will take anybody's handkerchief and hold it to his mouth, rub it vigorously with his hands while breathing on it, and immediately it bursts into flames and burns until consumed. He will strip and rinse out his mouth thoroughly, wash his hands and submit to the most rigid examination to preclude the possibility of any humbug, and then by his breath blown upon any paper or cloth envelop it in flame. He will, while out gunning and without matches desirous of a fire lie down after collecting dry leaves and by breathing on them start the fire.

Michigan Medical News, September 11, 1882

A similar case was reported in 1927, when Vice President of the US, Charles Dawes, is said to have personally investigated a car mechanic in Memphis, Tennessee, who supposedly had the mysterious power to set inflammable material alight merely by breathing on it. The man took General Dawes' handkerchief, breathed on it, and it caught fire. Dawes and his colleagues decided that it was no trick, and since no reasonable explanation could be found, it was left unexplained.

From May to July 1982, Scottish nanny Carole Compton worked in three different homes in Italy, and over a period of 23 days, five fires and various other poltergeist phenomena broke out in the houses. She was later arrested and spent 16 months in an Italian prison for attempted murder, though the charge was later dropped and she was found guilty of arson.

No inflammatory substances were ever discovered in any of the houses, and a Professor Vitolo went on record as stating that he was sure the fires were not caused by a naked flame, but by intense heat. The case of Carole Compton, the "nanny they called a witch," as the newspapers dubbed her, attracted enough attention to be made into a movie in 2003 called *Superstition*, starring Charlotte Rampling and Sienna Guillory.

If such incredible stories are genuine, how do we explain the phenomenon of pyrokinesis? In some fictional tales, pyrokinesis is described as the ability to stimulate an object's atoms, increasing their thermal energy until they burst into flames. However, scientists point out that without some form of electromechanical device which would release several of the compounds

known to spontaneously ignite upon contact with the oxygen in the air, or a triggering device positioned at the source of the fire, there is no known way to ignite a fire. Consequently, attributing pyrokinesis to some "unknown" power of the brain is simply explaining one unknown with another. Trickery, of course, should not be ruled out. Some researchers have suggested that A. William Underwood may have concealed pieces of phosphorus (which ignites in air at around about 86°F/30°C) about his person. As this temperature is just below body temperature, Underwood could easily have ignited the phosphorus by breathing or rubbing on it.

It is believed that Carole Compton was a victim of psychokinetic exteriorization, also known as a "poltergeist attack."

HOW TO

TEST FOR PYROKINESIS

1. HOW MANY PEOPLE ARE KNOWN TO HAVE HAD THIS POWER?

Though it sometimes appears in poltergeist cases, it is very rare.

2. HOW IS THE POWER ACQUIRED?

This power seems to appear spontaneously.

3. WHAT ARE THE EARLY WARNING SIGNS?

Unexplained fires breaking out in your vicinity.

4. HOW DO I KNOW IF I HAVE THE POTENTIAL TO DEVELOP THIS POWER?

If you have such a dangerous power you will know.

5. WHAT MATERIALS WILL I NEED FOR THE TEST?

A candle.

6. WHAT ARE THE DANGERS ASSOCIATED WITH THIS POWER?

All the obvious hazards associated with fires.

TEST

EXTINGUISHING A CANDLE

It is strongly recommended not to try any experiments connected with fire, although the following simple and safe test should not cause any problems.

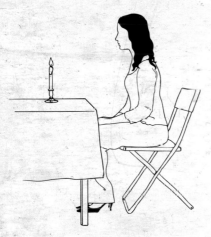

[1] Light a candle and sit down on a chair in front of it.

[2] Relax your body, focus, and concentrate on the candle. Nothing else exists except you and the candle.

[3] Mentally instruct the flame to grow taller. Visualize this happening in your mind.

[4] Next, try telling the flame to grow shorter, then to move to the left, then to the right.

[5] To extinguish the flame, imagine it dying down in your mind.

[6] To relight the candle focus intensely on it and imagine the energy surrounding it getting hotter and hotter until you are ready to instruct the candle to relight. You can also try and do this verbally, or by snapping your fingers, or clapping your hands.

CHARLES FORT

The following cases of unexplained fire starting were noted by Charles Fort. Unfortunately we do not possess much detail about the girls involved, so the cases, although intriguing, are unsupported by independent evidence.

In November 1890, in Thorah, near Toronto, Canada, strange things started happening around a 14-year-old English girl called Jennie Bramwell, the adopted daughter of a farmer, Mr. Dawson, and his wife. Bramwell reportedly fell into a trance, and cried out "Look at that!" while pointing to the ceiling which was ablaze. Shortly afterward, to the astonishment of Mr. and Mrs. Dawson, she pointed out another fire. The following day numerous fires broke out around the house; as soon as one was put out, another started. In one instance while Mrs. Dawson and the girl were seated facing a wall, the wallpaper suddenly caught fire. Bramwell's dress then burst into flames and Mrs. Dawson burnt her hands

extinguishing the fire. Fires continued to break out in the Dawson household for a whole week afterward. A report in the Toronto Globe, for November 9, 1890, described charred pieces of wallpaper, which looked as if they had been burned using a blazing lamp.

The situation became progressively worse, with the family apparently having to move all the furniture out into the yard. The unfortunate girl, blamed for the fires, was sent back to the orphanage from where she had come, and with her leaving, the phenomena stopped. The reporter from the *Toronto Globe* depicted her as "a half-witted girl [who] had walked about the house with a match, setting light to everything she came across." However, the reporter had difficulty explaining how the fire on the ceiling and those on the walls had been started. Charles Fort, describing the case, commented: "I'll not experiment, but I assume that I could flip

matches all day at a wall, and not set wallpaper afire."

The reporter also inquired whether Bramwell had any knowledge of chemistry, as according to him the "half-witted" little orphan was "well-versed in the rudiments of the science." He subsequently asked around town and apparently discovered that the girl had a reputation as a thief, and that she had visited the chemist numerous times on errands. In the opinion of the *Toronto Globe* the mystery was solved: the girl had stolen "some chemical" which she applied to various parts of the Dawson's house in order to start the fires.

In January 1895, fires broke out in the house of an out-of-work carpenter, Adam Colwell in Brooklyn, New York. The fires were investigated by police and firemen

who witnessed furniture burst into flames. They subsequently reported that they could find no cause of the fires. However, the Fire Marshall suspected the pretty adopted daughter of the Colwells, Rhoda, was partly responsible. He stated that he thought that Rhoda had started two of the fires, but not the others, as she was being questioned when some of them began. He had, he said, "no explanation to offer, as to the cause of the [other] fires or of the throwing around of the furniture."

Mr. Colwell stated that on the afternoon of January 4, while in the company of his wife and stepdaughter Rhoda, they heard a loud crash. A large, empty stove had fallen over and four pictures had fallen off the walls. Shortly afterward a bed caught fire, and a police officer who had been called to the house saw wallpaper start to burn. Another fire then started and a heavy lamp fell from a hook onto the floor. The house soon burned to the ground and the family, who had lost everything apart from

Above **In 1890, mysterious and unexplained fires broke out in a house near Toronto, Canada.**

their clothes, were taken to the police station. Captain Rhoades of the Greenpoint Precinct stated, rather prematurely as it turned out, that he could attribute the strange fires to "no other cause than a supernatural agency."

Some time later a Mr. J. L. Hope of Flushing, Long Island, came to see Captain Rhoades and told him that during the time Rhoda had worked for him as a housemaid, between November 19 and December 19, four mysterious fires had broken out. This evidence was enough to convince the Captain of Rhoda's guilt for the fires in the Colwells' house as well, and she was advised to own up. By now frightened at her situation, Rhoda admitted that she had started the

fires as she disliked the place where she lived and wanted to get away. The girl also stated that she had knocked the pictures off the walls and dropped lighted matches into the beds, continuing with her mischief even after the police, firemen and detectives arrived at the house. *The New York Herald* ran the story as "policemen and firemen artfully tricked by a pretty, young girl." The mystery solved, Captain Rhoades subsequently gave the girl some "wholesome advice" to which she apparently listened, and closed the case.

SEE ALSO

Poltergeist **Pages 160–162**
Pyrokinesis **Pages 179–183**

OUT-OF-BODY EXPERIENCES

Out-of-body experiences can be the result of the bearer possessing one of several "powers." They are grouped under this heading because they occur when a person's consciousness is said to leave the physical body and observe him or herself and the world from an external perspective.

ASTRAL PROJECTION

Astral projection, (also known as "astral travel"), can occur when the person is awake, during lucid dreaming (a state of dreaming while being aware you are dreaming), during deep meditation, while in an unconscious or semi-conscious state (due to shock or accident), or under the influence of drugs.

One of the earliest accounts of research into astral travel is Sylvan Muldoon and Hereward Carrington's *The Projection of the Astral Body* (1929). However, in the years following the book's publication, the term "astral projection" came to be regarded by parapsychologists as too esoteric and the alternative "out-of-the-body experience" was introduced in 1943 by G.N.M Tyrrell in his book *Apparitions*. However, the term "astral projection" is still used by some researchers today.

In esoteric teachings, such as those of the Theosophists, a nineteenth-century religious and philosophical group created by occultist Helena Petrovna Blavatsky (1831–1891), there is the belief that we have seven bodies (one for each of the seven planes of reality). According to this doctrine, during astral projection the astral body leaves the other six

Above left: Sylvan Muldoon.
Below left: Hereward Carrington.

bodies and journeys out on the "astral plane," while remaining connected to the physical body by a silver umbilical-type cord of infinite length.

While on a spiritual quest in the East in the 1930s, British philosopher, mystic, and traveler Paul Brunton (1898–1981), spent a terrifying night alone in the King's Chamber inside the Great Pyramid. Part of his experience was involuntary astral projection. In preparation for his ordeal, Brunton had fasted for three days before the experience to make himself more receptive to whatever might happen during his vigil. As he waited alone inside the dark chamber, in total silence and increasing cold, Brunton began to sense hostile forces around him, eerie shadows crowded in on

him from all sides, and a dark apparition seemed to advance menacingly toward him. All the legends of evil ghosts haunting the areas around the pyramids told to him by Arab villagers came rushing into his mind. But by a supreme effort of will Brunton managed to banish these terrifying images and, soon afterward, he was apparently visited by benevolent beings in the ceremonial dress of ancient Egyptian high priests, who led him through secret passages within the Pyramid to a great hall.

Inside the hall, Brunton lay down and immediately felt a kind of paralysis, as if his spirit was leaving his physical body and journeying to the "regions beyond death." His astral body passed upward through a narrow hole (as described in shamanic tradition) and transformed into a purely mental being with a sense of existence much more vivid than when in his physical body. Brunton describes looking down on his prone lifeless form and seeing a train of faint silvery light

Egyptian high priests in ceremonial dress led Brunton through secret passages within the pyramid to a great hall..

In Hart's collection of cases, about one in three people had undergone this type of OBE, where they had been seen by other people some distance from where their physical body actually was, or afterward provided a description of something they had "seen" which was actually happening at the time in the location they claimed to visit.

What is the explanation for astral travel—does it actually happen as Professor Hornell Hart believed? One hypothesis is that the human consciousness is a separate entity from the body, and can exist without the body (and the body without the mind), in other words, "dualism": the belief that the mind and body function separately, without interchange. Others believe that OBEs are the result of certain brain states triggered by illness or extreme stress. Skeptics point out that the evidence for astral projection and OBEs is all anecdotal, that while those claiming to leave their body may undergo some kind of "experience," the separation of mind and body is more likely to be hallucinatory rather than objective fact.

projecting itself from his spiritual to his physical body. He returned to normal consciousness quite suddenly, convinced that he had undergone some kind of strange mental initiation ceremony.

In a survey published in 1954, in the *Journal of the American Society for Psychical Research*, Hornell Hart, Professor of Sociology at Duke University, North Carolina, coined the term "ESP Projection." Hart used the term to refer to a type of out-of-body experience (OBE) which apparently provided evidence that the individual had undergone a real experience.

HOW TO

TEST FOR ASTRAL PROJECTION

1. HOW MANY PEOPLE ARE KNOWN TO HAVE HAD THIS POWER?

Quite a lot of psychics claim to have experienced astral travel (or out-of-body experiences—OBEs)

2. HOW IS THE POWER ACQUIRED?

Most psychics say they are born with it but it can be triggered by illness or extreme stress.

3. WHAT ARE THE EARLY WARNING SIGNS?

A "floating" feeling while on the verge of sleep, feeling "separated" from one's body.

4. HOW DO I KNOW IF I HAVE THE POTENTIAL TO DEVELOP THIS POWER?

If you have an excellent visual memory and a lot of imagination.

5. WHAT MATERIALS WILL I NEED?

None.

6. WHAT ARE THE DANGERS ASSOCIATED WITH THIS POWER?

Not being able to "re-enter" your body after astral travel.

TEST

DEVELOP ASTRAL PROJECTION

There are a number of methods you can use to begin developing the power of astral projection. However, trance-like states which involve fasting, solitary confinement, and mental strain, are not advised and may be injurious to your long term health.

[1] You will need to give astral projection your complete attention, so make sure you are alone and will not be disturbed. Sit or lay down on a soft and comfortable surface, and try to relax. Clear your mind, focus on your in-breath and your out-breath. You may start to feel sleepy.

[2] Provided you manage to stay awake, you will pass into a meditative state. This will take time and practice. When you are approaching the right state of mind, there will be a sinking feeling all over your body and you may feel like you are floating or walking down a flight of stairs. If you have trouble relaxing, you can use an aid. The most effective is the technique of binaural beats—recordings designed to help the mind reach optimum brain frequencies. These can be purchased online.

[3] As you concentrate on that sinking or descending feeling, the astral projection will occur when your brain finally just lets go. Many people report that their first out-of-body experiences last no more than about three seconds, so don't get discouraged. Over time, the more you practice, the more control you will be able to exert over your astral self.

[4] When you have mastered the practice of astral projection, you will be able to travel outside of your body virtually at will, but some people have had difficulty returning to the body. If you find yourself "stuck" in the astral state, there are a number of solutions: seek out a family member, whose familiar touch may help you rejoin the physical world; you cannot lose your body, but the feeling of detachment can induce panic, so calm down and you will be able to re-enter.

ROBERT ALLAN MONROE

Robert Allan Monroe (1915–1995), was an American businessman whose three books, *Journeys Out of the Body* (1971), *Far Journeys* (1985), and *Ultimate Journey* (1994), helped to popularize the concept of out-of-the body travel. Monroe's numerous and varied personal experiences of OBEs began in 1958 after he had been experimenting with data-learning techniques during sleep.

After one of his experiments he had a terrifying experience where he felt as if he had been seized by a "severe, iron-hard cramp." Over the next few weeks he had other unnerving experiences after his sleep-learning experiments, including one occasion when he felt he was floating near the ceiling and looking down on his sleeping body. Monroe's experiences of astral travel increased and broadened in scope, and he soon developed various techniques for leaving the body.

During his many OBEs, Monroe was able to identify three separate "dream worlds," which he termed "locales," and which he believed were extra dimensional. In his books, Monroe gives detailed descriptions of the properties of what he interpreted as the "second body." He states that this "astral body" has weight and can be seen under certain conditions, but is very plastic and can adopt any form that it requires.

Monroe was eager to discover the reality of his astral travel and the "locales" he visited, so began to develop techniques to allow other people to experience OBEs. In 1974 he set up the Monroe Institute in Faber, Virginia, a non-profit education and research foundation which offers "experiential education programs facilitating the personal exploration of human consciousness." At the Institute, Monroe developed a process called Hemi-Sync (short for hemispheric synchronization—Brainwave synchronization), a patented audio-guidance technology, which according to their website, www.

monroeinstitute.org, works by sending different sounds (tones) to each ear through stereo headphones. The two hemispheres of the brain then act in unison to "hear" a third signal—the difference between the two tones. This is not an actual sound, but an electrical signal that can only be perceived within the brain by both brain hemispheres working together.

Hemi-Sync technology has been commercialized and is available in the form of a series of audio CDs, offering a variety of applications for self-help, sleep, relaxation, stress management, and out-of-body experiences. After Robert Monroe's death in 1995, his daughter, Laurie A. Monroe, took over his role at the Institute until she also passed away in December, 2006.

Monroe has been criticized by skeptics for romanticizing and exaggerating his OBE experiences in his books. The journeys were, they argue, nothing but hallucinations, the product of

Robert Allan Monroe

Monroe's preoccupations, taking place inside his brain and nowhere else. As with the majority of "supernatural powers," scientists regard the evidence for astral projection as purely anecdotal or subjective, with no scientific evidence to back it up.

HOW TO

STUDY MONROE'S METHOD

Robert Monroe's 1971 book, *Journeys Out of the Body*, describes a rather long and complicated technique for inducing OBEs. Here is a simplified summary of Monroe's method.

[1] Lie down in a darkened room in a comfortable position, but with your head pointing toward magnetic north. Make sure you will not be disturbed.

[2] Loosen your clothing and remove all jewelry and metal objects, but you must make sure you keep warm.

[3] Begin by entering into a relaxing state of both mind and body. Then consciously tell yourself that you will perceive and recall everything that occurs during the upcoming process which will be of benefit to your being.

[4] Begin breathing with your mouth half-open.

[5] Enter the state bordering sleep, known as the "hypnogogic state," by concentrating solely on one particular object. When other thoughts start intruding and you lose focus, you have entered the hypnogogic state.

[6] When these other images start to enter your mind, watch them passively, this will also help you maintain this state of near-sleep.

[7] Begin to clear your mind and observe your field of vision through closed eyelids. Do nothing more for a while—simply look through your closed eyelids at the darkness in front of you.

[8] After a while you may observe light patterns, take no notice, they are only neural discharges which are of no significance.

[9] When these cease, you enter a deeper state of relaxation where you lose all awareness of the body and sensory stimulation. You are almost in a void where your only source of stimulation will be your own thoughts.

[10] With eyes closed, look out into the blackness at a spot about a foot from your forehead. Concentrate on this spot, and then move your consciousness to a point three feet away, then six, then turn it 90 degrees upward, reaching above your head.

[11] Mentally draw down the "vibrations" from this point above you into your body. You are now entering the "vibrational" state, sometimes indicated by a tingling feeling, as if electricity is rushing through your body.

[12] Learn to control the vibrational state by concentrating on the waves of vibrations and mentally pushing them from your head down through your entire body to your toes. Practice this process until you can perform it on command.

[13] Now you have control of the vibrational state you are ready to experiment with leaving your body. The most straightforward technique recommended by Monroe is the "lift-out." To employ this method imagine yourself getting lighter and of how pleasant it would be to float upward.

[14] Be sure to keep control of your thoughts and don't allow any extraneous material to enter your mind and interrupt them. You will soon find yourself floating upward above your body—your first OBE.

[15] With enough practice of this method, Monroe claims that a whole other world of experiences will open up to you.

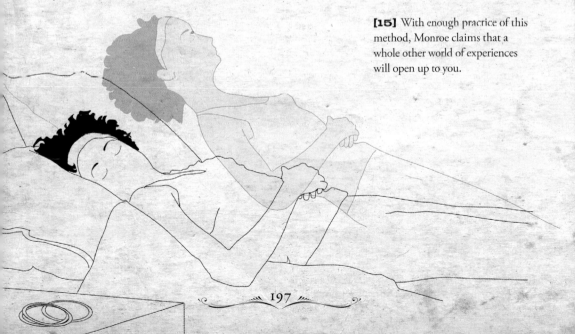

REMOTE VIEWING

Remote viewing is the ability to obtain information about a distant or unseen object, place, or person (known as the "target") using extrasensory perception. Since remote viewing involves a part of human consciousness leaving the physical body, out-of-body experiences and astral projection are also directly related to this "supernatural power."

Although there are one or two cases of what could be interpreted as remote viewing from the eighteenth and nineteenth centuries (see page 205), the phenomenon was not really studied until the 1970s. In 1974, parapsychologists Russell Targ and Harold Puthoff introduced the term "remote viewing" to describe their US government-sponsored work with "psychics" which culminated in a project known as Stargate.

Targ and Puthoff carried out their research into remote viewing at Stanford Research Institute (later called SRI International), Menlo Park, California. (SRI has no connection with San Francisco's prestigious Stanford University.) Remote viewers tested at SRI included former army "psychic spy," Joe McMoneagle, New York artist and psychic, Ingo Swann, and veteran psychic, Harold Sherman. The initial remote-viewing

Parapsychologist Dr. Russell Targ.

project had at least 16 psychics on the government payroll.

Part of the work at SRI was to train "psychic spies." Beginning in the late 1970s, a group of six such paranormal talents, known as "the naturals," was established. Claims were made that these remote viewers had a high rate of "hits," which included locating secret PLO training camps, finding American hostages during the 1979 Iranian hostage crisis, detecting a major Soviet submarine project, and finding the location of General Gaddafi of Libya. Far stranger were Ingo Swann and Harold Sherman's experiments involving remote viewing of the planets Mercury and Jupiter. Although Targ and Puthoff reported that the results of Swann and Sherman's remote viewing were in general agreement with the discoveries made by the Mariner 10 and Pioneer 10 research spacecraft, Swann's claim that

Above: Ingo Swann.
Right: 1979 Iranian hostage crisis.

experiments at SRI involved a person (known as the "beacon") going to a location unknown to the test subject, who would then be asked to describe or draw the locale. Later experiments refined the technique and involved giving only map coordinates to the psychic and requesting that they record their impressions of the unknown location. These impressions would then be compared to photographs of the actual locations.

Apparently, Ingo Swann provided some impressively accurate responses to the SRI tests which led, in part, to the US government-funded Stargate project, established to determine whether or not there was any potential military application of psychic phenomena. The Stargate project (or "operation stargate") was given a budget of around US$20 million, and operated from the National Security Agency's headquarters at Forte Meade, Maryland, for two decades. At one stage the

By remote viewing, Swann made reports on the physical features of Mercury and Jupiter.

there was a 30,000-foot (9,150-m) mountain range on Jupiter has been shown to be untrue. One particularly successful remote viewer at Stanford (she was said to have correctly identified five out of nine targets), was a photographer named Hella Hammid. One experiment with Hammid in July 1977 involved her being placed in a small submarine submerged in the Pacific Ocean two miles off the California coast. Hammid's "beacon" then went to a cliff above Stanford University and climbed a large oak tree. While in the submarine, Hammid said she was able to see a tree and a cliff, though she was not sure what activity her beacon was engaged in.

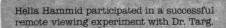

Hella Hammid participated in a successful remote viewing experiment with Dr. Targ.

even unclear, and their controls over experiments too loose. Since there were perhaps thousands of remote viewing experiments where the test subject would describe and/or draw a picture what appeared in their mind, it is to be expected that a number of them would resemble their targets in some general way. The SRI experiments did not require that the remote viewers give accurate descriptions of what they saw, consequently, a vague image could easily be interpreted by the judge (who always knew what the target was beforehand) as fitting a particular target.

Significantly, the US government discovered that "neither practice nor training consistently improved remote-viewing ability." Because the interests of the US government were in useful intelligence rather than scientific methodology, researchers at SRI did not hesitate in allowing the psychics access to as much background information as possible about the targets. Indeed when other researchers looked at Puthoff and Targ's data they discovered that their own students were able to work out the target locations by examining the clues that Puthoff and Targ had unintentionally included in the transcripts, rather than by employing any "psychic powers." Bearing this in mind, it is almost impossible to come to an objective opinion about the reality of remote viewing based on the research at SRI.

Does that mean, then, that there is no validity in the claims made by remote viewers like Ingo Swann? Being able to "see" hidden, distant locations does sound like the stuff of comic books, but if proven a reality, would have a profound effect on military intelligence, law enforcement, medicine, geology, anthropology, astronomy, and countless other disciplines. However, the fact that there are currently no known scientific projects researching the phenomenon of remote viewing would suggest that unless researchers come up with examples of this supernatural talent which can be repeated under strict laboratory conditions, then it will remain what skeptics term "pseudoscience."

Despite its initial promise, the Stargate project was terminated in 1995, mainly because remote viewing was too vague and unreliable to be of any use to the intelligence community. Targ and Puthoff's criteria for what constituted a "hit" during remote viewing experiments has often been criticized for being far too broad, or

REMOTE VIEWING RELATED POWERS

- ✪ OUT-OF-BODY EXPERIENCE (see page 186)
- ✪ ASTRAL PROJECTION (see page 188)
- ✪ TELEPATHY (see page 26)
- ✪ CLAIRVOYANCE (see page 36)
- ✪ DOWSING (see page 126)
- ✪ SCRYING (see page 136)

HOW TO
TEST FOR REMOTE VIEWING

1. HOW MANY PEOPLE ARE KNOWN TO HAVE HAD THIS POWER?

This is quite a rare power that was not really investigated until the 1970s, so few people are known to have demonstrated it.

2. HOW IS THE POWER ACQUIRED?

Remote viewers say they are born with the power, though it can apparently be developed further by training.

3. WHAT ARE THE EARLY WARNING SIGNS?

Images in your mind of distant locations, often places you have never visited.

4. HOW DO I KNOW IF I HAVE THE POTENTIAL TO DEVELOP THIS POWER?

You need an excellent visual memory and a lot of concentration.

5. WHAT MATERIALS WILL I NEED?

None.

6. WHAT ARE THE DANGERS ASSOCIATED WITH THIS POWER?

Don't delve into things you don't want to know about.

TEST

VIEW REMOTE TARGETS

Ask a friend to prepare a list of "targets," locations they have images and descriptions of that you do not know about:

[1] Relax and empty your mind of all thoughts, images, and feelings that are part of your normal consciousness. Try and do this for about five minutes.

[2] Visualize a black window in your mind. Try and prevent your imagination from putting familiar images (friends, your workplace) into this window.

[3] You will soon see indistinct images, shapes, and colors; patiently empty your mind of these images until you just see the black window.

[4] After ten minutes your friend will present a fact (known as an "identifier") about the target (for example, "it is close to the sea," "there is an old church nearby").

[5] Remain relaxed, with your eyes closed, and say the target identifier to yourself or see it written on the black window in your mind.

[6] Sit quietly and wait for visual details or feelings about the target to appear.

[7] After you receive the impressions, open your eyes and sketch the images or note down your feelings. You don't need to decide what the target is yet.

[8] Repeat steps 5–7 eight to ten times until you have a fairly full description of what you think the target is.

[9] Try the whole test again with a different target and compare how you do.

THE STORY OF BOTTINEAU

Not much is known of Bottineau, the obscure Frenchman who discovered the "science" of Nauscopie, that is, the detection of ships and lands at a considerable distance—up to 620 miles (1,000 km). He allegedly did this by examining the effect which they produced on the atmosphere—very much like an early form of remote viewing. He was supported by the concurring testimony of hundreds of people, and certificates from high-ranking officers all indicating that there must be some truth in his statements.

Bottineau relates in a letter that, as early as 1762, while serving in the French navy, he was thinking that a vessel moving toward land should produce a certain effect on the atmosphere, and so make the approach discernible to a trained eye well before the vessel itself was visible. After many observations, he thought he had discovered a specific appearance heralding the advance of a vessel before it came in sight. However, he had only limited success, and so gave up the idea.

In 1764, his career took him to the island of Mauritius (then known as the Isle of France), in the Indian Ocean, east of Madagascar, where he had a lot of free time, and again attempted to develop the art of "remote viewing." Here, away from civilization, with a clear sky, pure atmosphere, and fewer ships stopping at the island, he was less likely to make mistakes than off the coast of France. After six months Bottineau was sure of the reality of his discovery and of its value as a real science. He took advantage of the fact that officers were often on the shore looking through their glasses (small telescopes) for approaching vessels from Europe.

The island of Mauritius.

THE STORY OF BOTTINEAU

He made bets on ships arriving up to three days before they actually came in sight, and as he was very rarely wrong, he won a large amount of money, much to the bewilderment of the officers. The Governor of the island kept a record of Bottineau's remote-viewing predictions in a private register for about two years. On one occasion he announced to the Governor that three vessels were approaching the island, even though the lookouts could see nothing with their telescopes. The next day the lookouts told the Governor that a ship had just come into sight above the horizon. On the next day a second appeared, and a week later a third was visible to the naked eye. Bottineau's prediction had been correct. Though the government offered Bottineau a considerable sum of money and a pension for the details of his secret, he declined, saying that he didn't think the price high enough.

Incredibly, the Frenchman was allegedly able to detect the approach of ships from about 310 to 620 miles (500 to 1000 km) distant. For more than fifteen years he consistently predicted the arrival of vessels, at times three or four days before they could be seen with a telescope. The Governor's register showed that his predictions were nearly always correct; and that even when he announced the approach of vessels which didn't arrive at the island, it was shown that the ship or ships were foreign and had come within two or three days' sailing without stopping there.

On one occasion Bottineau claimed that a fleet of eleven vessels was approaching the island, causing great apprehension, as an attack from the English was expected. A warship was immediately sent out to check, but before its return, Bottineau informed the Governor that the signs in the atmosphere had gone, so the fleet must have taken a different 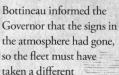 direction. Some time after this, a ship arrived in Mauritius from the East Indies, and reported seeing a fleet of eleven ships sailing toward Fort St. Williams. Again Bottineau had been correct.

Between the years 1778 and 1782, Bottineau correctly predicted the arrival of 575 vessels, several of them four days before they became visible to anyone else. At no time did any vessel reach the

island without first being predicted by Bottineau. Bottineau was also interested in whether the atmospheric effects produced by the approach of a vessel to land would be the same when one vessel approached another, and found that when he tried the experiment during a voyage, the effect was the same, though less powerful. He also wanted to try his method out in discovering land from a ship long before it could normally be seen from on board the vessel. On one occasion he told the captain of a ship he was traveling on that they were within about 90 miles (150 km) of land. The captain refused to allow this possibility but, after re-examining his calculations, was forced to acknowledge

that he'd made a mistake, and changed course immediately. Bottineau discovered land three times during the voyage, once at the distance of 450 miles (750 km).

In June 1784, in the midst of the French Revolution, Bottineau went to Paris to try and get some official notice for his new science. But perhaps because people had little time or inclination to think of such things, he was practically ignored, even though he had certificates signed by the Governor of Mauritius, and all the officers of the garrison there. Bottineau was ridiculed by the editor of the *Mercure de France*, saying that it was not "ships at sea, but castles in the air" he'd seen. He was completely disheartened by this rejection and predicted that the world would be deprived of his discovery. He was right, the world did not listen, and he died in poverty in the (at that time) French colony of Pondicherry, southern India, around 1802.

In 1817 and 1818 Captain Francis Maude of the Royal Navy

Above **The seizure of the Bastille during the French Revolution, 1789.**

(1798–1886), at the time a midshipman on HMS *Magicienne*, often met an old inhabitant of Mauritius who had learned the art of Nauscopie from Bottineau himself, and used it regularly with great success. More than a century later, in 1935, Peter Green, of Tristan da Cunha, an island in the Atlantic between South Africa and South America, was also attributed the ability to predict the arrival of ships one or two days in advance.

SEE ALSO
- - - - - - - - - - - - - - - - - - -
Clairvoyance **Pages 37–44**
Precognition **Pages 49–54**

BILOCATION

There are a variety of names for the "double," the type of apparition which appears to be the ghost of a living person. One closely-related term is "bilocation," which is used to describe a living person who is reported to be in two different places at the same time; and on a number of occasions the double is actually mistaken for the real person. The double of the living person behaves in a somewhat mechanical way and usually does not respond when spoken to. Often the double is interpreted as a harbinger of bad luck and even a sign of the imminent demise of the person whose apparition appears. This latter characteristic links the double closely to "crisis" or "death bed" apparitions, where a person either dying or under immense stress, appears in ghostly form to a relative or close friend.

Similarly, the doppelgänger, a German word which translates as "doublewalker" or "doublegoer," signifies an apparition which acts in the same way as another person. The doppelgänger often haunts its living counterpart, behaving as an "evil twin," and is also known as a "fetch" or "wraith" in British and Irish folklore. Doppelgängers were sometimes believed to have been switched at birth, the good child being replaced by an evil one. It is believed that if the two should ever meet, then they will both die.

A man haunted by his own ghost.

On Holy Thursday, 1226, St. Anthony of Padua was preaching in the Church of St. Pierre du Queyroix at Limoges, when he suddenly remembered that he was supposed to be present at a service in a monastery at the other end of the town. St. Anthony slowly pulled his hood over his head and knelt down for some minutes in front of the congregation. At the same moment the assembled monks at the monastery chapel witnessed the saint emerge from his stall, read the appropriate passage, and immediately disappear.

Another example of saintly bilocation concerns St. Alphonsus Maria de'Ligouri, who on one occasion on September 21, 1774, fell into a trance after saying Mass. When he came out of the trance, which is said to have lasted a day and night, St. Alphonsus explained how he had visited the bedside of the dying Pope Clement XIV, at least four days' journey away. It was

Above: St. Ambrose of Milan it is believed had the ability to "bilocate."

The ability or phenomenon of bilocation, where the individual appears to divide themselves in two, is one of the rarest of paranormal abilities, although it has a long history. Over the centuries, claims have been made that bilocation has been practiced by gurus, mystics, magical adepts, monks, and saints. Indeed it is in medieval Christian literature that we find some of the earliest references to bilocation. Some Catholic authorities believe that the ability to "bilocate" was bestowed upon a number of Christian saints, mystics, and monks, including St. Ambrose of Milan (338–397), St. Severus of Ravenna (born c.348), St. Anthony of Padua (1195–1231), and St. Pio of Pietrelcina (also known as Padre Pio, 1887–1968).

Above: Pope Clement XIV was visited by St. Alphonsus while he was in a different location.

friend's. One wet summer evening, Goethe was out walking with a companion in Weimar when he suddenly stopped and began talking to someone visible only to himself. His companion, who saw nothing, became more worried as Goethe proceeded to address his friend "Frederick"—asking him why he was out on the highway dressed in Goethe's own dressing-gown, night-cap, and bedroom slippers. Worried that the apparition might be some kind of portent for the death of his friend, Goethe rushed home to his lodging only to find his friend sitting in an armchair. Frederick explained to Goethe that he had arrived at the lodging soaked to the skin by the rain and had changed into Goethe's night clothes. Falling asleep in the chair, Frederick had dreamed that he had gone out to meet his friend who had spoken to him in the same words that Goethe had used to the apparition on the highway.

Above: Padre Pio is rumored to have been in two places simultaneously, using the power of bilocation.

later revealed that the Pope had died at seven o'clock in the morning, the exact moment when St. Alphonsus emerged from his ecstatic state. Apparently on several other occasions credible witnesses stated that they had seen St. Alphonsus in two different locations at the same time.

Accounts of the life of Padre Pio, even those which bear the "Nihil Obstat" of the official Roman Catholic censor, include incredible stories of bilocation, when the Padre is believed to have been in two places simultaneously. Examples include him appearing to Italian soldiers in North Africa in the Second World War and attending bedridden women, when he was known to be in the cloister.

Reports of bilocation are not confined to catholic saints. German visionary and author of *Faust*, Johann Wolfgang von Goethe (1749–1832), once saw his own double or doppelgänger, and on one occasion, a

Above: Goethe had an encounter with his friend's doppelgänger.

In Welsh folklore, the doppelgänger is known as "the lledrith," which means "illusion." The lledrith never speaks and is supposed to vanish if spoken to. In the past this apparition was often regarded as a death omen, though, as the following example illustrates, this was not always the case. The following tale, told by Marie Trevelyan in her *Folk-Lore and Folk-Stories of Wales* (originally published 1909), is from near Talgarth, a small market town in southern Powys, mid Wales:

A young man... said he once chased his wife for a mile and a half up hill and down dale, until he panted for breath, and was forced to halt, when she vanished. Thinking all this was done for a frolic, he went home, to find his wife quietly seated by the window, knitting. "How did you get back?" he asked. "Get back?" reiterated his wife. "Why, I've never been anywhere!" "Tut, tut! Gwen," said her husband. "You looked as roguish as could be beckoning me from the cherry-tree and out into the road. Then you ran, and I followed a mile and a half, until I could follow no more. I was forced to sit down." "Then you must have followed a Lledrith looking like me, for I have not been outside the doors since you went to the barn after tea."

(*Folk-lore and Folk-Stories of Wales*, 1909, pp193–4.)

As can be seen from the selection of cases presented here, bilocation can be both voluntary and involuntary. In many stories an emotional crisis or need seems to have resulted in the apparition or phantasm of the real person manifesting itself. In the Sagée case (see page 216), as in many others if the stories are to be believed, the double appears to draw its strength to manifest from its human original. This characteristic has caused some researchers to compare this aspect of bilocation with the exhaustion experienced by materialization mediums after they come out of their trance. Although the double occasionally seems to serve a purpose (there are instances of it advising its original on the right decisions to make, for example), there often seems to be no purpose involved in the appearance of the double.

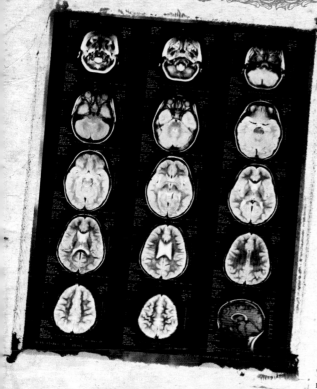

Can visions of doppelgängers be reproduced by electromagnetic stimulation of a patient's brain?

have that someone is standing next to us when there is really no one there. The doctors carried out experiments with a 22-year-old woman with no history of psychiatric problems, and who was at the same time undergoing presurgical evaluation for epilepsy treatment. Arzy and his colleagues stimulated a certain spot in the woman's brain with electricity and found that, as in certain aspects of the case of Emilie Sagée, the patient described an imaginary illusory or "shadow" person which closely echoed changes in her own body position and posture.

Arzy and his team have posited that disturbance of a site on the brain's left hemisphere induces the uncanny sensation that there is a double lingering nearby. However, Arzy's theory of an apparition triggered by the brain cannot explain all cases of the double, for example, those where the double was supposed to have been witnessed by others. Nevertheless, Dr. Arzy's fascinating research certainly indicates that some reports of bilocation may have their origin in the left temporoparietal junction of the brain.

Skeptics would argue that the evidence for bilocation consists merely of hearsay, or second- or third-hand reports. To the doubters, it is another example of pseudoscience, and rather than study stories of bilocation, skeptics suggest that investigations should be made into the psychological state of those who commonly have such experiences. However, there has been some recent scientific work that suggests a curious psychological aspect to the doppelgänger, or double, phenomenon.

In September 2006, the journal *Nature* published a paper by Dr. Shahar Arzy and colleagues from the University Hospital, Geneva, Switzerland. This paper proposed a cause for the eerie feeling we sometimes

BILOCATION— RELATED TERMS

- ✪ ASTRAL PROJECTION
- ✪ CRISIS APPARITION
- ✪ DOPPELGÄNGER
- ✪ DOUBLE
- ✪ EVIL TWIN
- ✪ FETCH
- ✪ LLEDRITH
- ✪ PHANTASM
- ✪ WRAITH

HOW TO
TEST FOR BILOCATION

1. HOW MANY PEOPLE ARE KNOWN TO HAVE HAD THIS POWER?

It is a very rare power, mainly associated with a number of Christian saints and mystics.

2. HOW IS THE POWER ACQUIRED?

This is a mysterious congenital condition which has rarely been traced back to a specific moment in the life of those possessing it.

3. WHAT ARE THE EARLY WARNING SIGNS?

Voluntary and involuntary "splitting" into two separate entities.

4. HOW DO I KNOW IF I HAVE THE POTENTIAL TO DEVELOP THIS POWER?

If you possess the power, it will be obvious.

5. WHAT MATERIALS WILL I NEED?

None.

6. WHAT ARE THE DANGERS ASSOCIATED WITH THIS POWER?

There are none, but you may be considered strange if you practice this power in public places!

TEST

DEVELOP BILOCATION

There is no known way to develop a power as bizarre as bilocation. However, since in many respects it is a similar ability to astral projection and out-of-body experiences, it may be helpful to refer to the astral projection test described in this book.

EMILIE SAGÉE

The most famous case of bilocation is undoubtedly that of Emilie Sagée, recorded by politician, author, and spiritualist, Robert Dale Owen in his book *Footfalls on the Boundary of Another World* (1859). The story was told to Owen by a Latvian aristocrat named Julie von Güldenstubbe.

Below **Emilie Sagée and her doppelgänger.**

From 1845–1846, Emilie Sagée, a 32-year-old French-born school teacher, was working at "Pensionat von Neuwelcke," an exclusive girls' school near Wolmar in present day Latvia. Von Güldenstubbe had been a pupil at this school when she was 13 and related to Owen the bizarre things that occurred around Sagée. Apparently the school teacher had caused much consternation around Pensionat von Neuwelcke by often being seen in two places at the same time. On one occasion when Sagée was writing on the blackboard in front of 13 students, her exact double appeared next to her and proceeded to mimic her actions, though it was not holding any chalk. At dinner one evening, a similar incident occurred when Sagée's double appeared behind her copying the movements of her eating, although it held no utensils. Sometimes there was a considerable distance between Sagée and her doppelgänger.

On one occasion Sagée was seen in the school's garden gathering flowers, while another teacher sat on a chair supervising the entire body of 42 pupils, who were together in the school hall for their sewing and embroidery lessons. Suddenly, Sagée's double appeared in the teacher's chair while her "real" self could still be clearly seen outside in the garden. The students away. When these instances of bilocation occurred, Sagée would become weaker and more rigid, while the double became more defined and consistent. Sagée stated that she was always unaware of the manifestation of the double.

According to von Güldenstubbe, Sagée was well thought of as a teacher, but the directors of the school had no choice but to end her contract when parents, hearing of her strange reputation, began to withdraw their daughters from the school. Apparently Sagée had lost 19 other jobs in 16 years because of the sudden appearance of her "double."

The Emilie Sagée case is one of the most fascinating in the paranormal canon, though a word of warning. The only first-hand source for the story is a single witness, Julie von Güldenstubbe, 13 years old at the time of the strange events, and whose testimony was recorded 14 years after the incidents are said to have occurred.

noticed that while the double sat motionless in the chair, Sagée herself moved around in a rather tired fashion out in the garden. Apparently, two girls plucked up the courage to touch the ghost in the chair, and felt a slight resistance. One of them then even stepped in front of the chair and walked right through a part of the apparition, before it slowly vanished

Above **Sagée's double would appear in front of pupils.**

SEE ALSO

Astral projection
Pages 189–193
Bilocation **Pages 209–215**

FURTHER READING

Dunne, J.W., *An Experiment with Time* (1927, A&C Black)

Flournoy, T., *From India to the Planet Mars*
(1994, Princeton University Press)

Fort, C., *The Complete Books of Charles Fort*
(1974, Dover)

Goethe, J.W., *Faust* (1962, Anchor)

Kilner, W.J., *The Human Atmosphere, or the Aura Made Visible by the Aid
of Chemical Screens* 1911. Reprinted as *The Human Aura*
(1965 Citadel Press)

Korotkov, K., *Light After Life: A Scientific Journey into the Spiritual World*
(1998, Backbone Publishing Co.)

*Light After Life: Experiments and Ideas on After-Death Changes
of Kirlian Pictures* (1998, Backbone Publishing Co.)

Moberley, C. A. E., and Jourdain, E. F., *An Adventure*
(First printed in 1911 by Faber)

Moses, W.S., *Spirit Teachings*
(2009, Kessinger Publishing)

Moss, T., *The Body Electric: A Personal Journey into the Mysteries of
Parapsychological Research, Bioenergy, and Kirlian Photography*
(1979, J.P. Tarcher)

Moss, T., *The Probability of the Impossible: Scientific Discoveries and Exploration into the Psychic World* (1974, J.P. Tarcher)

O'Donnell, E., *Haunted Places in England* (2003, Kessinger)

Ostrander, S., and Schroeder, L., *Psychic Discoveries: Behind the Iron Curtain* (1984, Prentice Hall)

Owen, R.D., *Footfalls on the Boundary of Another World* (2010, Spaight Press)

Philippe, J., *Prince of Aesthetes: Count Robert De Montesquiou 1855–1921* (1968, Viking Press)

Randi, J., *Flim-Flam!* (1982, Prometheus Books)

Roberts, J., and Butts, R. F., *Seth Speaks: The Eternal Validity of the Soul* (1994, Amber-Allen Publishing)

Robertson, M., *Futility: Or the Wreck of the Titan* (2006, Filiquarian Publishing)

Stead, W.T., *From the Old World to the New* (1892, London Review of Reviews)

Trevelyan, M., *Folk-lore and Folk-Stories of Wales* (2006, Kessinger Publishing)

Worth, P., *Hope Trueblood: A Nineteenth-Century Tale* (2008, Kessinger Publishing)

Worth, P., *Telka: An Idyl of Medieval England* (1928, Patience Worth Publishing Co. Inc)

Worth, P., *The Sorry Tale: A Story of the Time of Christ* (1976, Health Research)

Yost, C.S., *Patience Worth: A Psychic Mystery* (2005, Kessinger Publishing)

INDEX

INDEX

INDEX

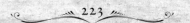

CREDITS

All other images are the copyright of Quintet Publishing Ltd. While every effort has been made to credit contributors, Quintet Publishing would like to apologize if there have been any omissions or errors—and would be pleased to make the appropriate corrections for future editions of the book.

T = top, L = left, C = center, B = bottom, R = right, F = far

Andrew Skolnick: 120TR.

IStock: 124.

Mary Evans Picture Library: 7B; 9B; 14 © SPR; 17B; 18T; 19T; 19B © Harry Price; 28L © Guy Lyon Playfair; 30TL, 33CR © Stacy Collection; 34TR © Rue des Archives/Tallandier; 34BL © SPR; 45TR; 46R; 48; 52B © SPR; 55TR © Harry Price; 56BL; 59B © SPR; 60; 61, 64TR, 64BL © SPR; 66; 68TL © SPR; 70BL © Harry Price; 73TR © John Cutten; 74; 76 © Guy Lyon Playfair; 78; 79 © Harry Price; 83TL © Illustrated London News Ltd; 94 © Guy Lyon Playfair; 96; 97B; 98TL; 100T; 100B; 103; 109TL © SPR; 117CR © Rue des Archives/Tallandier; 126; 129BL; 135; 136; 138TL; 145BL © Malcolm Greensmith Collection; 145 FB; 154; 156; 157B; 165TR © Manfred Cassirer; 166BL © John Cutten; 168 © Guy Lyon Playfair; 178; 188; 189BL; 202TL © John Cutten; 207 © Rue des Archives/Tallandier; 209B; 210BR; 211TL.

Photo of Robert A. Monroe is reprinted by arrangement with Monroe Family, LLC: 195.

Rex Features: 179B © Courtesy Everett Collection/Rex Features.

Shutterstock: 2; 6; 7T; 8; 10TL; 10TR; 10B; 17T; 18B; 18BA; 21; 22R; 24BR; 25; 27T; 28R; 30B; 33B; 35T; 35CR; 36; 38TR; 38BL; 39TL; 39BR; 39FR; 40TR; 41TR; 41CL; 41BR; 45BR; 46TL; 49T; 49B; 50; 51T; 51CL; 51B; 52TR; 57BR; 58; 65; 68BR; 69CR; 60B; 77B; 82BL; 84BL; 84R; 85BR; 86; 87B; 88R; 89TR; 89TL; 90; 99T; 99B; 104; 105TL; 105TR; 105C; 108T; 109BR; 112BL; 112BR; 113TR; 113BL; 116L; 116R; 117BL; 120BL; 121; 122TR; 123R; 128TL; 133TR; 133BR; 134TR; 134BL; 137B; 138BL; 141TL; 142; 143; 144; 146BL; 146TR; 147R; 151TL; 151CL; 151BL; 151BR; 152TR; 152BL; 153TR; 153BL; 158BL; 159BL; 160TC; 160TR; 162; 165BL; 166TR; 167; 170T; 171T; 171B; 174BL; 174BR; 175TR; 175BR; 176TR; 176TL; 177; 179C; 181TR; 181BL; 181BR; 184; 185; 186; 191T; 191B; 198; 200TR; 201T; 201BL; 202TL; 205; 206; 209C; 212B; 213; 216TL; 217TR.

Topfoto: 9T © KPA/HIP; 12T © Fortean; 12B © Fortean; 16; 22BL © UPP; 23 © ImageWorks; 24TL; 26 © Fortean; 27B © Topham Picturepoint; 29 © Fortean; 37B; 39BL © Topham Picturepoint; 40BL © The Granger Collection; 47TR © RogerViollet; 55BL © Fortean; 56TR © Ullstein Bild; 67B, 69TR © The Granger Collection; 70TR © UPP; 82 CR © Topham Picturepoint; 93, 95 © Charles Walker; 98BR, 106, 107B © Fortean; 112TR © Topham/AP; 115B © The Granger Collection; 127B © Fortean/Aarsleff; 128CR © The Print Collector/HIP; 130TL; 147L; 158TL © Topham Picturepoint; 158TR © Fortean; 159TR © From the Jewish Chronicle Archive/HIP; 160B © Fortean/Webster; 161 © Fortean/Playfair; 169B; 174T © Topham Picturepoint; 180TR; 189BC © Charles Walker; 190, 199 © Fortean; 200B © The Granger Collection; 201BR © Fortean; 208; 210TL © The Granger Collection; 211BR © R.Feltz.

Zedcor: 37C; 59C; 67C; 77C; 87C; 97C; 107C; 115C; 127T; 137C; 145C; 157C; 169C; 189C.